THE
FRONTIERS
OF
PARADISE

THE
FRONTIERS
OF
PARADISE

*A Study of Monks and
Monasteries*

PETER LEVI

WEIDENFELD & NICOLSON
New York

Published by Weidenfeld & Nicolson, New York
A Division of Wheatland Corporation
10 East 53rd Street
New York, New York 10022

First published in Great Britain in 1987
by Collins Harvill.

Grateful acknowledgement is made to the BBC and
Anvil Press for permission to reprint "Ruined
Abbeys" (Appendix), and to Longman Group Ltd for
permission to reproduce the map on page 61.

Library of Congress Cataloging-in-Publication Data

Levi, Peter.
    The frontiers of paradise: a study of monks and
monasteries / Peter Levi.—1st ed.
        p.   cm.
    Bibliography: p.
    Includes index.
    ISBN 1-555-84197-X
    1. Monasticism and religious orders—History.
I. Title.
BX2461.2.L48 1988
255'.09—dc19   87-33977
                                                      CIP

Manufactured in the United States of America

First American Edition, 1988

10 9 8 7 6 5 4 3 2 1

For Deirdre
For January the 11th

CONTENTS

INTRODUCTION

On the day I finished writing the rest of this book, I read in *The Times* that a novice monk who was an ex-paratrooper had been sent to prison for a year by a court at Bordeaux for selling off the furniture of the monastery. I once knew a novice who chased another one with a carving knife; he caught him too. These are not the worst stories I know about monks by any means. A few years before 1914, the Russian monastery on Mount Athos had offered sanctuary to so many criminals on the run that they took it over, and very nearly got control of the entire Holy Mountain. The Greeks naturally complained, and Russia sent a large warship into the Mediterranean. The monastery refused to surrender and had to be stormed by marines. If any of the wicked ex-monk, ex-criminals survived another four or five years in Siberia, one wonders what happened to them in 1917. Nor is this the oddest story about monks.

At first one thinks the interesting thing about monks is, what do they actually do? What are the details of their daily life? The more one goes into detail about that, the more differences appear between places and between historical periods. Perhaps a history of monks might be the solution? But it is such a vast subject, and so entangled with world history, and the details are so complicated to explain, that the history of monasteries cannot be reduced to one simple or readable book. On the other hand, an unhistorical book about monks would be useless and insipid. What I have chosen to do is to discuss the most important historical turning-points in some detail, but to show as much as possible by examples, which have been picked for the light they shed on this or that.

Monks are not confined to Christianity, nor to the Middle Ages, nor to Europe. I have tried to compare and contrast all kinds, to see

9

what they have in common, to discuss their various roles in their particular societies, and so to come at suggestions as to what they are, what their motive is, and what makes a monk be a monk. I have paid particular attention to the position of women, to monks as others see them, and monks as they see themselves. I have been as objective as possible. There is no part of this book which presupposes the truth or superiority of Christianity or of any religion. Our history is simply what happened, and monasteries were a rather unexplained part of that history for a long time. As a phenomenon in common between so many different cultures and historical periods, monks suggest a type of unity in the history of the world, or a large part of it, at a certain stage of the development of human nature, which is not often observed. But the differences they suggest are even more interesting, and I have often concentrated on those.

There is a difficulty of definition. Monks, loosely defined in the West, live enclosed in monasteries for the rest of their lives, bound by vows and supervised by their churches. But there are Buddhist monks, Indian monks, hermit monks and communities of hermits, wandering monks and innumerable kinds of nuns. I have taken a wide definition wherever the outer, blurred edges threw light on the centre, or on some important historical current that affected the centre. But I have followed the centre itself, particularly in Europe, in much more detail. That is partly because it is more knowable.

I have been well acquainted with monks, nuns and friars all my life, and lived for a time in a religious order with enough monastic features in its training to give one a certain inwardness with monasteries. I have never met an Indian hermit, but otherwise I have at some time come across all the kinds of people I talk about, hermits included, with the obvious exception of people of earlier times.

One of the strange things about monasteries is the similarity of motive, of character, and of activity, that can easily be observed across many centuries. Monks alter more slowly than, let us say, soldiers, even though in every generation they bear a certain mark of their historical period.

This book took a very long time to think about and to write, and it relies on many years of desultory researches before that. It relies on tottering piles of other people's books, but I do not think it is at all like any single one of them. This is chiefly because I have tried to treat monks as a worldwide historical phenomenon, and to discuss them honestly and respectfully, but without dogmatic prejudice of any kind. I have no idea whether they have any future. Readers must decide for themselves.

Part 1

*

Monks

Monkishness

To the question, what are monks like? I have found to my surprise that the answer is curiously simple. They have a great deal in common which cuts across differences of rule, culture, climate, language and religious belief. I recollect an odd scene in Oxford when Buddhist monks, knowing very little English, settled like swans on water in complete sympathy and understanding with English monks. Indeed, it was the English who looked slightly awkward, out of politeness. Elderly Greek monks are recognizably similar to the monks of Tolstoy's Russia, but so one might expect. They are also very like the monks one will meet in any provincial monastery in the West. It is the elderly inhabitants of the monasteries who are similar: the younger ones have more in common with the outside world of their generations, and therefore less with one another.

What marks the monks in the course of their long lives is a silence of the spirit, a childish innocence, an apparently meaningless goodness. They become like good children playing at being good. Their simplicity is more obvious than their depth. Their ceremonies are second nature to them, and they perform them with reverent relish, though by no means always with a young man's exactitude. These good old men have always given me particular pleasure, but if a novice realized that the vocation of a young monk is to become an old monk, I think he would be terrified. Of course there is an analogy with ordinary family life. But through celibacy, community isolation, and the long, sober intoxication of prayer, the monks in old age develop the kind of eccentricity that Oxford dons used to exhibit before they were permitted to marry. Old monks are wild as well as simple. They perch more lightly on the globe than the rest of us.

This is best explained in anecdote. These events have stuck in my head for a lifetime. They are not the matured fruit of reading, but stray fragments of real life.

On a long walking tour in Crete we came at last to a monastery on the south coast. It was ancient and magnificent, but nearly empty. Most of it was occupied by a police garrison, who had a telescope trained on some rocks across the bay, where hippies were said to swim naked. We found that orders had been given that no hospitality was to be offered to travellers, and of course there was no inn within two hours. The oldest monk sat with us on a bench in the dying light, wagging his white beard. He explained his profound mistrust of Western Christianity, his chief objection being which shoulder they touched first in the sign of the cross. When darkness had fallen he brought us a secret feed of more lettuce than we could eat, out of his private garden, and a large bag of rusks. He was a very real old man. After the fall of Crete to the Germans that monastery sheltered thousands of defeated soldiers; they got away in submarines from the creek.

Once I came across a retired abbot, straying around a religious building. He was on his annual outing from a remote country monastery in the English midlands. He was elderly and bright-eyed, with apple cheeks; he could almost have been a retired general, or a simpler, happier younger brother of Thomas Hardy. He was wholesome and extremely charming. I asked him about his life and he told me about his visions, the first one in the fields that had called him to the monastery, and others later, that seemed to him familiar and unremarkable. They did not sound like stories he had told before, and I have no doubt about his absolute truthfulness to experience. I did not probe or interrogate, which is why he was so confident. He said how he longed for the final, everlasting vision, which could not be long delayed.

He had advantages of nature and temperament, as well as grace, which we are told builds upon nature. And he was old. Ageing contemplatives often foretell their own deaths to the day, even the hour, and foresee it with tranquillity. My own great-uncle, who was a Dominican of no famous distinction, did so with perfect accuracy and against medical opinion. His last words, when the brethren crowded round his bed on that long-predicted festival of the Virgin, were "Heavens, the death of Nelson". On the other hand, I remember the death of an old Jesuit of some sanctity. It was thought that he did not realize he was dying. The Rector of the house tried to explain it to him, and asked if he had any last request. He asked for a new pair of boots. He died in a few days as he had always intended, and was found to have put his papers in order. It is not at all unusual for these dying old men to show the mild and gleeful naughtiness of children. That is not, of course, unique to monasteries. I particularly enjoy the last words of a religious who, being told he was dying, said, "Well, I've nothing to fear, I've never been a Superior."

The active middle age of monks is often less attractive. They have a strength of spirit and of bone which might be mistaken for worldly confidence. It inspires awe rather than affection, and sometimes a certain pity. Here again there are worldly analogies. But it may well be that these men are themselves only alone or in choir, at their prayers. What they know that no one else knows is perhaps known only then. Middle age is not the natural climax of life, not even of monastic life, and freedom of the soul may often mature only with the senility of the body. "These old men are like medlars, they are never ripe till they be rotten," Shakespeare says. How very much less admirable is the development of writers, who are never ripe till they be written.

I am not old enough to have known any monks from youth into old age. But I have known some over thirty years, and the process of maturing leading to a modest spiritual authority is both usual and remarkable. It is unlike any normal success in life, and seems rather to be based on an early acceptance and digestion of failure with a subsequent diminution of the ego. The temptation of Thomas in Eliot's *Murder in the Cathedral*, about doing the right thing for the wrong reason and so on, belongs to an early stage of religious life, though no doubt the same crisis may recur, particularly after a powerful middle age of worldly activity. One of the worst cankers of monastic life is a disguised ambition that recurs when religious certainty has hardened into complacent self-righteousness. This leads to a lack of kindness and a stubborn narrowness of view, all too often to be observed in monastic history. Outright corruption is much less dangerous to the spirit.

It is sometimes thought, because of the lack of biographical and autobiographical sense in the writings of long periods of the Middle Ages, that the monks of that classical age stood still among the timeless machinery of the soul. But to stand still is the one thing a monk cannot afford to do. He must develop, however slowly, under the rule of life he has chosen, or he will go backwards. The same is probably true of communities, hence the restless struggle for reform. The life of a monk within his monastery is in many ways unnatural. It is a traditional artifice, and even a small fault in that can throw it off balance. It goes without saying that it depends on a traditional or proverbial wisdom, and on a traditional belief outside the monastery. When that decays or alters for better or worse, the monastic life will take a new form, or it will wither away in time. Monasteries have often been missionary enterprises, but they have always depended on a solid tradition of belief centred on Athos, on Rome, on Ireland, on the cave sanctuaries of Afghanistan, on some kind of mother country of monks.

Thomas Merton is a modern case worth considering. He was a young intellectual American with European experience. He was perhaps a poet who had lost his way. There is an unpurged vulgarity about his conversion. "Thick flakes of golden fire flashed from the shadowy flanks of the upturned chalice. My heart was ready to explode." By extreme antithesis to his earlier life and his apparent temperament, he became a Trappist, he entered silence, physical severity and painful routine. One can see in the long series of his writings as a monk, how that life blossomed for him. He conveys the physical quality of monastic life, with its frugal but all-important consolations, better than any other writer. He drinks blackberry juice and watches the sky and the country in perfect

18

peace, meditating on the commentaries of Gregory or the mystical meaning of the prophets. Then one feels that he wrote too much, having been ordered to do so, and came close to writing himself out of his vocation. He became a hermit, returned to poetry, saw visitors, travelled, and electrocuted himself by accident in a shower-bath in south-east Asia.

One may reasonably conjecture that he should have been left alone in his monastery, but who can say where a human life will take one, and who can say what is the will of God? Will the monastic form ever digest the wave after restless wave of modern humanity? And if not, must it define itself as anti-modern? The extreme relaxation of liturgical solemnity can hardly suit the ceremonies and conventions of a monastery, one might think. A scholar of the history of the Trappist Order was shocked not long ago to see the liturgical readings of the office performed by a young American in jeans and a checked shirt, with his hands in his pockets. One can have no view in principle about that, but it does raise the question whether changes in the Church may not prove more momentous for monks than those changes in the world that brought them about. For better or worse, English monasteries depend for their growth and stability on monastic schools and old-fashioned parishes. One does not know how long that kind of education can last. Or how long our kind of human society will last.

Monasteries

At any visitor's first entry into a monastery, time seems to stand still. If one spends a week in one or a month, a different scale and pattern of time imposes itself, which at first one resists as if one were in prison. When this new time-scale is accepted, it soaks into one's bones and penetrates one's mind. It has nothing to do with death or eternity, but it involves a tranquil, unhurried, absolutely dominating rhythm. This specially undisturbed yet specially rhythmical sense of time is the greatest difference between monastic life and any other. Beyond the rhythm of days is the underlying rhythm of seasons and festivals. The liturgy sets the pace: above all, the night hours and early morning hours. No one, as David Knowles remarks, can really understand the monastic vocation who has not seen the sun come slowly up at the end of a long night office, through the great east window of an abbey church.

The office itself is a long, long series of psalms and readings interspersed with prayers, all chanted in Latin at set times of the day. The longest part is matins, the night office that has dawn for its climax. The noise of monks chanting is like the musical moaning of the wind or the sound of waves on pebbles; the higher voices of nuns are like the buzzing of flies perfectly orchestrated. The most musical monastic chanting I ever heard was the thrilling bass polyphony of Bulgarian monks. The dominant style in Western Europe is that of Solesmes, which is exquisitely controlled and modulated, though it has to my ear a sea-sickening smoothness. The Italians by contrast have an unregenerate peasant musicality with some peculiar nasal noises of their own. The Germans are dramatic, with plenty of dark tones. The English are brisk and businesslike.

The control of time that music always imposes while it lasts extends in the liturgy through a variety of antiphonal responses to a completely shared experience. It is far easier and more deeply moving to sing the liturgy than to listen to it. This rhythmic, controlled time is closely tied to the natural cycle of day and night, to recurring Sundays and the seasons of the year: that love which moves the sun and the other stars is so expressed. It also extends through the day by routine and the sounding of the abbey bells. Though not all monasteries keep precisely the same hours, and although the hours may vary by season, and may have altered in the course of monastic history, the underlying presence of a rhythm musically expressed and utterly dominant in life has never ceased.

Western monastic architecture, with its tall bell-towers, its severe and regular pillars that seem to be assembled by sober music, its sober cloisters and high windows is obviously the product of this same rhythmic sense. Somewhere on a well-shaft in a monastic cloister I remember the words, *O sobria ebrietas, O ebria sobrietas*: O sober drunkenness, O drunken sobriety. Even the water and the light and darkness are mystical symbols, and real ones. They are part of one long, inexorable drama. All this seems more marvellous and more strange to us than it would have done in the past, because much of human life was once determined by the rhythms of days and seasons. In the late nineteenth century in certain English villages, people were still summoned to the fields by the church bell, or on estates by a stable bell. In France the angelus punctuates the day. In the Middle Ages words like prime and matins and vespers came to indicate the time of day by reference to the sun, without referring to the precise time of clocks, so that it is sometimes hard to know at what time by our clocks the offices were actually sung.

Both the basic symbolism I have mentioned and the sense of a vast swing of stellar and solar time of which each season's passage and each day's passage were small images, and which was marked by festivals of the year like the small landmarks of every day's liturgy and routine, are much older than Christianity. Virgil is conscious of this sense of nature, of the heavens, the earth, and human nature on the earth. The discovery was not classical, it is rooted in the nature of the year, of animal life, and of agriculture. "Lenten is come with love to town" is the statement of two very ancient aspects of the hungriest season of the year.

Monasteries make the whole of life an extended musical drama. This drama is one in which the monks take part with their entire lives: it is built around their deepest religious mysteries, and it mysteriously releases the soul. Every monastery in the world of whatever religion has its own ritual monotonies, and its own monotonous music, its own ceremonies of light and darkness and water.

The drama brings nothing about except for the individual soul, though it is always thought to have some connection with a spirit world. Christian monks pray for the souls of the dead and guard their relics. The friends of Epicurus pursued philosophy free from worldly care, in mutual charity. The followers of Plato and Aristotle pursued the mind's journey to God in the same place for nine hundred years. Christianity and the Dark Ages built up a liturgy and an architecture, with all the bells and black robes and processions and lights and hymns instead of work-songs, which dramatize these pursuits to the monks themselves and to their audience, to ourselves. When Patrick Leigh Fermor approached La Grande Trappe in failing light in a broken-down butcher's van across a storm-stricken heath, the deathly notes of an angelus echoed above the storm. *Les moines se couchent*, said the butcher. The sight of the vast Tibetan monasteries on their peaks, as it is still preserved in old photographs, is awe-inspiring. They are other-worldly in the same way that Everest is.

The familiar can become loved and revered, but it no longer inspires awe. One comes to know every stone of one's abbey, comes to be a senior monk, to view the state of the chant or the roof as a sailor views an elderly ship, but God does not cease to inspire awe, and by extension the liturgy, in its slow transmutations, embodies both God and nature; because it is seasonal, it is inexhaustible. The readings do not come round too often, and the psalms are long. The principal study of young monks used to be to learn the psalms and the chants and the rituals by heart. Down to the tenth century very little was written down; the continuity in the life of monasteries depended largely on oral transmission, as most life did. The writing and illuminating of manuscripts began to play a greater part in Benedictine life only when the thirteenth-century intellectual movement in Europe, which fell largely into the hands of the friars, transformed the life of the Church. Conservative monks opposed the change strongly since it meant reducing the time spent in formal prayer for the dead and for benefactors. They thought it showed ingratitude, lack of propriety, and that nemesis would follow and had followed.

There are two problems here. One is that contemplation is individual and wordless, and the other is that not all monks were or can ever have been intellectuals. Even the new theology of such masters as Thomas Aquinas, which spread quite fast through monasteries, was not to everyone's taste, though its procedures were amazingly tranquil and its conclusions nourishing and undisturbing by modern theological standards. It is possible to maintain that from the time when, by a long drawn out process, intellectual life in Europe broke free of monastic serenity, the monasteries were doomed to become backwaters. But their purpose is prayer, and the learning, the study and the philosophy that prayer demands. Of course no study can remain within self-imposed limits. The old monasteries would have been appalled by the hard-headed studies of some modern monks; they would not have trusted modern Oxford or Cambridge. And monks still tend to study the Bible and the liturgy, and their own medieval traditions. If they can do even that properly by modern scientific standards, it is a great achievement. The nuns often manage better than the men at the study of art or literature.

The combination of repeated verbal prayer with some direct attention to God's presence must remain a mystery to outsiders. Buddhist prayer techniques include the constant repetition of a simple phrase. The phrase can even be put into a wheel which one turns and turns. A similar repetition was and still is common in Greek monasteries. The recurring refrains of all the Christian liturgies, and the Roman Catholic rosary, have a quality which is not dissimilar. When the psalms are chanted, one cannot dwell constantly on the meaning of the words, they are too rapid.

It must always have been true that some of the words, being in a dead language, meant little to many monks; what is worse, some of the phrases of Jerome's Latin are virtually unintelligible in themselves and far from expressing what the Hebrew psalms originally meant. Yet the mysteriousness of the liturgy has always been one of its essential qualities. It is a rhythmic inducement to the soul, lulled from distractions and absorbed in music, to approach God.

This has to be experienced, not explained, but those whose whole life it is are often satisfied. They know the full force of a river that most of us have never entered and few of us have ever observed.

The Setting

The agricultural wealth of monks and the peasant basis of their lives is not God-given. As a phenomenon of Western social history the same conditions affected everyone. Even the hospitallers of St Antony who cured skin-rashes all over the Mediterranean had the right that their pigs, which followed them about, should forage freely in the streets, like Indian holy cows. Even the religious military orders, of whom I have written nothing, because they were rather soldiers than monks, however bound by their vows, and subject to more alarming corruptions than the simple inhabitants of the abbeys, had lands and rents. The monks on the whole acquired them gradually. The English Benedictines began to exploit and oversee their lands for themselves only in about 1200. In 1066, after all, there was little exportation of food from its area of production, the village was the unit, and few of the towns were big enough to have any need of a market. Monasteries let their land on long leases, often of two lifetimes.

But they had sheep. At the time of Domesday Book, Ely alone had 13,400, in 1125 Peterborough had 1,439, and nearly a thousand sheep grazing on the Essex marshes belonged to foreign abbeys. Those who are lucky enough to have eaten Romney Marsh lamb will remember the taste of marsh herbs. Lamb from the *prés-salés* is valued in France. The huge flocks increased by leaps and bounds. In 1252, Glastonbury had 6,717 and in 1320 Winchester had 20,000, Christ Church Canterbury had 13,730, and Peterborough and

Crowland had 16,300. Only the biggest of the sheep-crazy Cistercian abbeys had more. I assume that this enthusiasm for sheep arose because wool had a market, and sheep-raising was not labour-intensive. The grazing grounds were often distant. Glastonbury had flocks in Wiltshire, and Pershore had them at Broadway, but other flocks went farther. As for the income, the Glastonbury accounts show it going back into the land, and into dovecotes, dairy farms, and barns, as well as into vestments and books and monastic buildings. Every six ewes needed an acre.

When prices began to rise in the twelfth century with the growth of markets, leases began to be called in and shortened wherever that was possible. Accounts were drawn up showing the milk yield of ewes and cows and the economics of seed corn. Christ Church Canterbury had four copies of the book *Husbandry*, by Walter of Henley. They turned to corn-growing, because that was where profit lay. At Glastonbury they reclaimed wasteland and embanked against the sea. They bought land and fought land cases in court. By the eighties of the thirteenth century, the Archbishop of Canterbury was attacking the system of monks living as wardens in scattered manor houses, but without much success. By that time the greater abbeys ran their land with different specializations in different estates, rather like varied holdings in the stock market. This is the weight under which the medieval Benedictine monasteries sank.

It has its sympathetic side. Even their poetry was rustic, when it was any good. Thomas of Hales in the mid thirteenth century wrote one of those medieval lamenting poems about mortality and the famous dead, "Where is Paris and Helene?" The first stanza ends, "He has glided out of this realm, as the sheep has from the hillside".

> Hi beeth y-gilden ut of the reine
> So the shep is of the cleo.

As for their music, it had scarcely altered from 1000 to 1200, and probably not for two hundred years before that. Its notation, which mostly appears in the tenth century, was so simple as to allow room for tradition and for improvisation. It must constantly have been refreshed by country voices, and the echoes of country singing styles. One of the first recorded English songs, from a Reading monastic manuscript of about 1240, is "Sumer is icumen in". It was sung as a round. At that time the *conductus* began to be sung; it began as processional music, in which a tenor sang to a new tune or a popular song tune, and other voices sang in descant. It sounds rustic enough.

The Calling

The monastic ruins that first made me think about monks are extremely quiet places. The first article that ever I wrote was entitled "Study to be Quiet"; it appeared in the *Downside Review* just as I was going up to Oxford as an undergraduate. This title was taken from Izaak Walton on fishing, but came originally from St Paul. I was interested in a streak of contemplative quietism in seventeenth-century English poetry, which I then took to be in some way a result of the abolition of monasteries. Some need, or at least some habitual craving which lasted a generation or two, was going unsatisfied now that monasteries were not there to meet it. I think I derived my view from Christopher Devlin, who was then finishing his life of Robert Southwell.

One would be hard put to it to verify whether the view was a true one, and personally I was probably more interested in pastoral poetry, privacy and the limiting of ambitions. That interest arose not only from literature, but from the conditions of my own life. In a certain sense this book is an extension of the old article. But one could add to the material it first covered in a number of ways. If there was any thirst for loneliness, seriousness and contemplation, it must have been personal to individuals, and there did exist in that period Catholic monasteries abroad and Anglican communities in England, including the Fellows of Eton in the days of John Hales, whom Aubrey discovered there "drinking madeira and reading the Imitation of Christ", where one could have led a monastic kind of life. "He loved canary; but moderately, to refresh his spirits." But truly monastic life is not what poets usually want, though it might satisfy a craving they express: one among many cravings after all. In reading about Little Gidding I always have a sense of some element of play-acting.

And it is not really monasteries on the whole that obsessed English poets or most others, but hermitages. I do not think this was simply for romantic reasons. The human need that draws certain temperaments to extremes of isolation and religion and attracts many more at certain times or in a certain measure, is older than organized monasteries in the West, and independent of them in India to this day. It goes deeper. It survived the dissolution of the monasteries, which at the time of their dissolution had become rambling institutions sheltering many different kinds of men and women. The good hermit in Shakespeare is a converted or a repentant figure who has turned away from the world; he may be modelled on the Emperor Charles, or more remotely on the legend of Guy of Warwick. The friar in *Romeo and Juliet* comes from Renaissance Italian plays, and the only true monks I recollect, unless "bare ruined choirs where late the sweet birds sang" refers to monks, are the rich ones mentioned by the Archbishop of Canterbury in *Henry V*, an essentially ridiculous personage: though I have sometimes imagined that his bees, "the singing masons building roofs of gold", might be monks in their monasteries.

Hermits figure in other poems not by Shakespeare. One of the most memorable of these allusions is "calmer far than in their sleeps forgiven hermits are". That sets the slightly unreal tone very accurately. No one in England was going to become precisely a hermit, though Thomas Bushell, a servant of Bacon, lived as a hermit for seven years on the Isle of Man, so Aubrey says. The economic and social conventions would not permit it. A hermit would presumably have been prosecuted as a sturdy beggar, let alone a heretic. But it remains fascinating to see in more detail how poets imagined the hermit's life which they imagined they were longing to lead. Thomas Lodge (1558–1625), son of a Lord Mayor of London and by profession a doctor of medicine, wrote a *Commendation of a Solitary Life*, printed in 1589. He also wrote *Old Damon's Pastorall*, which is almost equally sententious. His *Glaucus and Scilla* is supposed to have suggested Shakespeare's *Venus and Adonis* and it has been argued that Lodge was the prototype in real life of the melancholy Jacques. He did retire to the country where he had at least a conversion of seriousness, probably under the influence of Robert Southwell, a genuinely contemplative saint.

> Sweet solitary life thou true repose,
> Wherein the wise contemplate heaven aright,
> In thee no dread of war nor worldly foes,
> In thee no pomp seduceth mortal sight,
>> In thee no wanton ears to win with words,
>> Nor lurking toys, which city life affords.
>
> At peep of day, when in her crimson pride
> The morn bespreads with roses all the way
> Where *Phoebus* coach with radiant course must glide,
> The Hermit bends his humble knees to pray:
>> Blessing that God, whose bounty did bestow
>> Such beauties on the earthly things below.
>
> Whether with solace tripping on the trees
> He sees the citizens of Forest sport,
> Or midst the withered oak beholds the Bees
> Intend their labour with a kind consort:
>> Down drop his tears, to think how they agree,
>> Where men alone with hate inflamed be.
>
> Taste he the fruits that spring from *Tellus* womb,
> Or drink he of the crystal springs that flows:
> He thanks his God, and sighs their cursed doom
> That fondly wealth in surfeiting bestows:
>> And with Saint *Hierom* saith, *The Desert is*
>> *A paradise of solace, joy, and bliss.*

This mild, attractive poem has a final stanza so lame I have not quoted it, yet its lameness is crucial to my argument. He prays in it "that I may leave the thought of worldly things" and for nothing more concrete.

> Then in my troubles will I bless the Time
> My Muse vouchsafed me such a lucky rhyme.

It is as if his mind had wandered or his spirit had gone off the boil, because he dared not confront what at some deep level he was looking for. I do not think monastic life would have been a true solution for the problems of such a man. In about 1600 he married. He died of plague in 1624, and his wife survived him.

The cult of the hermitage tails off into mere pastoral and repentance into mere grief, a willow-cabin at thy gate.

> I an old turtle
> will wing me to some withered bough, and there
> my mate, that's never to be found again
> lament till I am lost.

The Ruins

We are not able to see the ruins of monasteries with the eyes of the sixteenth century, and we cannot cut away any part of our history. If we seek pure and immediate communication with some past age, we shall be deluded. The suppression and ruination of the monasteries in the Reformation was viewed with grief, superstitious fear and rage. These feelings entered into proverbial language. When Shakespeare spoke of boughs that shake against the cold: bare ruined choirs where late the sweet birds sang, the monasteries had cast a shadow. Donne compares the mortal human body to a house that will fall "to dilapidation, to ruins, to rubbidge, to dust". Some unknown hand inscribed a poem in the ruins of Melrose Abbey.

> The earth goes on the earth glittering in gold,
> The earth goes to the earth sooner than it wold;
> The earth builds on the earth castles and towers,
> The earth says to the earth, All this is ours.

The ruins have been sanctified by time, they have lost the clear edges of their specific meaning, they have become a general symbol of mortality. The old antiquarian Sir Henry Spelman could still devote a book to the awful revenge of God, by which no family that had taken over monastic estates or built its house of the monastery stones prospered there for long. But he belonged to the Catholic minority, and his powerful book was misconceived. Some families prospered for generations on monastic lands, though among that social class which most acquired such royal favours it was not at all uncommon to suffer a grisly fate in the next hundred or so years.

To us the ruins of monasteries have an extraordinary and immediate beauty, whether they stand now in some great private park as Bolton Abbey does and Fountains once did, or in the middle of industrial towns. The context of later history is to them like the afterlight of a past thunderstorm.

Of one abbey in Normandy in a beech forest, nothing is left but one great lichen-greened, sun-gilded pillar, standing in a field. Abbey Dore in the middle of a working farmyard, Minster Lovell by its quiet stream and Tintern Abbey beside a road crowded with coaches in an elbow of the Wye Valley, have utterly different personalities, more so now in all probability than when they flourished within their own estates, but the beauty and the residual meaning of these places survive. The massiveness and the delicacy are both reduced to extremes, and the unworldliness intensified by ruin. Not even municipal or ministerial uniformity can take away their desolate magic.

The sentimental and romantic view of monks and monasteries that Walter Scott takes in his poems is nowadays even more unintelligible than the furious grieving of Sir Henry Spelman, and much more so than the simple desire to record, to immortalize the lost state of things, which inspired the other early antiquarians. The attractions of romance did exist: they were felt in the influence of Spenser. But they did not at first extend to monasteries. Before the Reformation the Nativity was already being painted in a Gothic ruin, but it was not monastic. Aubrey referred not to a monastery but a castle as "a very romancy seat". Monastic ruins had no connection with medieval romances, and began to seem romantic only when they began to seem fantastical. Then at once they became landscape decorations and garden ornaments. Shenstone had an artificial hermitage at the Leasowes, and Stourhead had another. Pope imagined the land "where slumber abbots purple as their vines". To the Protestant English travellers of the eighteenth century in Europe, monks and monasteries were objects of curiosity. The monks at Calais made a particularly lamentable impression.

One must not forget that great abbeys survived in use, and even monks were not unknown to the English Catholics of that age. One of Dryden's two sons appears to have died mad as a monk, living secretly at Canons Ashby. These boys were partly educated at Rome. The diarist John Evelyn records soon after the death of Charles II that Dryden was seen going to Mass with his two sons and Nell Gwynn. Perhaps it was all part of not letting poor Nellie starve. As for the abbeys, we still have some of them. Canterbury, Winchester, Bath and the rest are the most solemn and moving monuments of our history. The boys' dormitory of Westminster School is or was the old monastic granary of the Abbey. Tewkesbury is as fine as any abbey in Normandy, in the classic Norman manner. Cirencester has some relics of its monastic housing. But my own prejudiced pleasure is most intense at Malmesbury, for its simplicity and its mixture of ruin and reality.

That is because the ruins of monasteries speak more clearly than the real, inhabited places. I find the same to be true of Buddhist sanctuaries. They preach a stronger sermon, their voices being silent. They summon more urgently having fewer things to say.

They have sharpened their paradoxes, about God because they make no human sound, about death because they are empty and one can see light through them and they summon up their dead, and about nature, because having been artefacts of elaborate grandeur they have gone back to being natural objects, blown through by the wind and sometimes overgrown or grazed by cattle.

I have never been quite certain to what extent monasteries existed physically for the sake of outsiders. The founders would not have thought so. Yet the handsomest Spanish and Italian monasteries seem to rear up like stage scenery, like something imagined, like the sketch of an ideal. To become a monk or a hermit is to dramatize oneself, as Shakespeare and Scott realized. In their daily life were the monks dramatizing themselves for one another's sake, or communally for a communal self-image, or were they really doing it in some way for the others, for those outside the walls? Psychological states do exist in which one might play out some long drama for the sake of those who would never see it. If this is an ingredient in the life of monks, and if the silence they enter when they say, I will go unto the altar of my God, is meant to be a silence overheard by us, and haunting us, then its strongest effect is attained not in the realities but among the ruins of monasteries.

I have printed as an appendix to these rather heady statements the verse script of a television film about Cistercian ruins in Yorkshire which I made twenty years ago with Mischa Scorer. In some ways it is sharper, more lucid and full-blooded than this book, which is meant to complement it.

Part 2

The History of Monks

The East

I am forced to introduce the part of this book most concerned with history by admitting to uncertainty, but history depends on its available sources, and these are better and fuller in some areas than in others. Everyone admits that the earliest monks we know of were Indian, but the remote origins of their movement are unknown. Everyone agrees that Buddhist monks in all their sub-forms derive ultimately from Indian examples, but very early Buddhist history is not well documented, and I am incompetent to trace what happened in Japan, which I have never visited, though I have met and been much impressed by Japanese monks. There is a worse problem. It is tempting to suggest that Christian monks derive from the Indians or the Buddhists by way of Syria and Egypt, but not a shred of hard evidence has been discovered that this is really what happened. If the reader finds this state of our knowledge unsatisfactory, I can only agree. It is simply that the Western records are fuller and often more reliable than the Eastern.

The basis of Indian monasticism is the rejection of this world: Hinduism is a religion deeply rooted in one kind of society, and what it promises is deliverance. That is the doctrine which was spiritualized by Gautama Buddha, the teachings of whose disciples strayed this way and that, and came to include an admixture of Greek philosophy, which they inherited from the Romans in India or the Greeks in Afghanistan and southern Russia. Oriental monasticism achieved a flourishing period in Tibet, where between the seventeenth century and the twentieth a fifth of the population were monks, and another in Ceylon, where abbots were judges and ministers of state. Western European monks were most numerous between the eighth century and the eleventh, Russian monks between the thirteenth century and the fifteenth. But it does not make sense to call this a single historical movement. It is one phenomenon only in the sense that revolution is one phenomenon; it is not one movement.

Buddhist monks were casteless, though they soon began to reject the blind and lame (ordinary beggars) and the wicked. They dressed from the beginning in the red or reddish-yellow of Indian ascetics. They did accept nuns, but very reluctantly. Their rule was that a nun even a hundred years old must still rise from her seat to salute the youngest of monks. The Indian *math*, or monastic community, had been small; just a little circle of huts or cells. By the second century BC the Buddhist communities were populous. Their simple principles were to be truthful, honest, restrained and liberal and to do no harm to any living thing. There can be no doubt that a certain earthly compromise, involving the cult of relics and a magnificent art that went with the relic-shrines and ran riot in cave-sanctuaries and finally in temples, had something to do with their success. And they wandered a long way, so far indeed that their foreign wisdom greatly impressed the people among whom they settled. When the Buddhists with their fine art and medical science reached China, monks in the West were still balancing on lonely pillars and nesting in the branches of trees. This latter class are called Dendrites; they sound charming, but alas we know very little about them.

Solitaries

The monastic movement in Europe began in the Egyptian desert in the third century AD. Before that time we hear of various wild and bearded sages and miracle-workers, prophets and mystics, in the pagan world. Plutarch and Lucian knew of them, and they appear on the margin of the New Testament and more substantially in the Old. The difference is that in Egypt they developed communities of their own, with austere rules and traditions that were written down, under the government of abbots. In fact they lost their wild, extreme and marginal character and became institutions. Congregations of loosely grouped hermits were replaced by organized communities living together. In the fully developed monastic system, the life of the spirit is all but mechanical, and the desert survives only in the heart.

Hermits have numerous motives and impulses. Third-century Egypt was not a happy place. The early Christian hermits were refugees from the climax of pagan persecutions, and from central authority in all its forms. At the same period the archaeology of Western Asia shows the people of the towns moving out into small settlements in the countryside to avoid the taxes and burdens of citizen life. Diocletian's decree on wages and prices was part of an attempt to avoid wholesale desertions from organized Roman life, which was hellish. In Egypt there was nowhere to go except the desert. The sun blazes there all day, intensely expressing to the lonely soul the presence of God and God alone. The asceticism of the early hermits had roots in philosophy, in dramatized sexual self-denial, and in the tortures and martyrdom that had become the destiny of urban Christians. The Donatists, a sect that arose in North Africa with the freedom of the Church, were ruthlessly unforgiving to any Christian who had ever compromised with the pagan state.

The life of Paul the first hermit and that of Hilarion of Cyprus were written by Jerome, the most brilliant literary figure of the age, a strong supporter of monasticism and sexual abstinence. They are improbably romantic. The hermit Paul lives in a deep grotto where an opening to the air reveals dripping water and a palm tree. This hideout was used by forgers of false coinage in the days of Antony and Cleopatra. One imagines a small deserted mine. When Paul meets the hermit Anthony, a raven drops them a loaf of bread. When Anthony dies, the lions of the desert dig his grave and Paul buries him. Hilarion lives in an old abandoned orchard by a mountain temple of Venus haunted by devils, "so as to have his enemies at hand". The famous stories of the temptation of Anthony in the desert are more romantic still. Yet Jerome was about fifteen when Anthony died in 356: the garden of mythology had flowered swiftly. Jerome's life of Paul was intended to compete with the life of Anthony by Athanasius, which was written in Greek and Latinized by Evagrius of Antioch. Jerome has Paul bury Anthony in a cloak provided by Athanasius. Alas, mythology spreads and overwhelms everything. In later versions Anthony travels; he reaches Barcelona, and the Devil-Queen tries to marry him.

The truth so far as we can know it is threadbare but more interesting. Anthony was an abbot, and with few exceptions the Egyptian hermits must always have been organized in communities and attached to the outskirts of more normal human societies. Anthony was born in Upper Egypt in 251, and joined a local group of desert holy men in 271. From 286 when he was thirty-five he lived twenty years as a hermit alone, in the abandoned fortress of Pispir. Enough must have grown in it to supply his frugal physical needs. He kept up a garden of some kind, and he made and sold mats. In the course of those twenty years disciples gathered round him, and in 306 he left his lonely hideout to be abbot of a monastery and guide its younger men. He visited the city of Alexandria to give courage to the Christians there in 311, and again as a sage to argue against heretics in 355, being then 104, a year before his death. If one is disposed to doubt his long life, which would of course explain his great authority, it is the earlier dates that must be adjusted. He might have joined the local holy men as a young boy, like Daniel the Stylite. Even Benedict makes provision for the offering of a child to the monastery.

The rule of the wise old abbot (from *abba*, father), whose wisdom was mystical and based on his experience and simple integrity, was a dominating factor in the early development of monastic ideals in the West. It still plays a part, though the wisdom nowadays is largely of a different kind. The traditional instructions, and even a sermon by Anthony which may be genuine, can be recovered from the writings of Cassian and to a lesser degree from the *Lives of the Desert Fathers*. They are simple, austere and frequently charming, sometimes humorous. Since these writings have always been popular among religious communities, the entire Western tradition has been constantly sprinkled from that ancient desert water-spring. The wisdom of the past has always to some degree mitigated or inspired the understanding of written rules. The monastic study of the past is not narcissistic, it is a matter of identity and essential at all times.

Hilarion (about 290 to 370) was from Gaza, and became a Christian as a student at Alexandria. He visited Anthony and learnt from him. His parents died, and he gave away everything and set himself up as a hermit at Majuma in Palestine. That is supposed to have happened in 306, the year that Anthony left Pispir. He lived in a reed hut, then in a cell, four feet or so by five, surrounded by men and women disciples and visited by crowds. He fled to Egypt, then to Sicily, then to what is now Dubrovnik, and finally to Cyprus, at first to the orchard at Paphos, and finally to a remoter place, where Epiphanius the Bishop of Salamis knew him, and buried him, and wrote his life. That biography is lost now, but it was the foundation of the small masterpiece by Jerome. The dead body of Hilarion was dug up again and taken back to Majuma, to that first community of monks he had deserted for their own good, and for their greater peace and quiet.

The rule based on personal wisdom has largely survived in Buddhist monasteries, in the Zen monasteries that still flourish in Japan and in the pure air of the monasteries of Kashmir and Nepal. There is no simple general reason why monasticism grew up in so many places in the same period, but it is notable that its principal early centres were subject to late Roman influences while being more or less free from Roman power, on the margins of the Empire. This is true of India and Afghanistan, of Ireland, and of the Egyptian desert. What is in common appears to include a certain philosophized monotheism, and a sense for remote and marginal places of refuge, one might almost say outlaw country; a rejection of the civilized world. Hilarion buzzed about the Mediterranean like a bee in a bottle.

What happened in India was both the same and different. Friedhelm Hardy demonstrated twenty years ago that the early Indian mendicant monks were first of all mendicants, who met in certain caves to take shelter together in the rainy season. The caves became their monastery and their home. When one reads the *Questions of Milinda*, and the stories of vast assemblies of Buddhist monks in Afghanistan, at places like the refuge valley of Bamyan which is honeycombed with caves, one gets a similar sense of missionary pilgrimage and return to base. It was the monks who carried Buddhism to China along the silk roads, and Chinese Buddhist monks on pilgrimage to the home shrines provide our best records of what Buddhist Afghanistan was once like. It must be important that all over the world the life of monks and the existence of shrines of pilgrimage are closely intertwined.

One of the crudest examples of that connection is Glastonbury, where the monastery burned down, and the lucky "discovery" of the grave of King Arthur the past and future King was part of a fund-raising campaign. Even the bones of Anthony, who was buried by his own wish in an unmarked grave, were "rediscovered" in the sixth century: later they turn up in Alexandria, in Constantinople, and at La Motte. The cult of the Apostle James at Compostela began with the discovery of a Roman marble sarcophagus, which it was locally assumed was too grand to contain anything less than an Apostle. The relics in Buddhist stupas descend to such strange objects of veneration as some bristles of a brush with which the Buddha swept the floor. The most truly spiritual example of the pilgrim element is to be found in the writings of the Japanese priest and poet, Basho, a delicate and intense travel record.

> In this mortal frame of mine which is made of a hundred bones and nine orifices there is something, and this something is called a wind-swept spirit for lack of a better name, for it is much like a thin drapery that is torn and swept away at the

slightest stir of wind. This something in me took to writing poetry years ago. . . . The grassy hermitage of Saigyō was about two hundred yards behind the innermost temple of Yoshino. It was separated by a steep valley and approachable only by a narrow trail covered with leaves. The famed spring was just as it had been, shedding its clear drops of water with a drip-drop sound. . . .

The *Memorandum on Buddhism* written by Han Yu in the early ninth century is animated by his fury about relics.

> And now your majesty, I hear that you have ordered all Buddhist monks to escort a bone of the Buddha from Feng-hsiang and that a pavilion be erected from which you will in person watch its entrance into the Imperial Palace. You have further ordered every Buddhist temple to receive this object with true homage . . . this absurd pantomime. . . . The Buddha was born a barbarian; he was unacquainted with the language of the Middle Kingdom, and his dress was of a different cut. His tongue did not speak nor was his body clothed in the manner prescribed by the Kings of old. . . . I beg that this bone be thrown into water or fire.

His grave Confucian anxiety that Buddhism might be a herald of other and disastrous foreign influences and invasions was justified by events. The contempt for monks and for their holy relics has often been echoed in the West, but in the early ninth century no imperial Roman conservative was left alive quite as civilized as Han Yu.

Egypt

Writers often suggest that the disorganized hermit movement in Egypt drifted vaguely and rather late into communities, and was regulated largely when it reached Europe, first by the rule of Basil in Greece and then by the great Benedict. But everything in the history of monasteries is more complicated than it looks, even in the Egyptian desert. There were two ways of life there from a very early stage, and in both of them the personal motives and qualities of those who withdrew from the world were extremely varied. Some fled from persecution, some from authority, some pursued virtue, some God. Since Egyptian Christianity was or became Monophysite, that is they believed Christ was God but not man, his humanity an illusion or phantasm, there were special grounds for mysticism in Egypt. Whether the mysticism followed the belief or vice versa, I am unable to say. The two ways of life in the desert derived from Anthony and from Pacomius.

Anthony's tradition began simply as the independent hermit with a group of disciples nearby; the hermit would die and be buried in his cave, and a community might continue to exist around the holy place. Anthony himself disliked this prospect; hence his secret burial. In the course of time these communities drifted closer together, at first to have a church in common. Gradually walls appeared, small boundary or garden walls. Slowly from the fourth century to the ninth centralization increased, though little groups of disciples gathered round a master were still to be found not far from the monastic centre. When the Arab invasion was imminent, watch towers of mudbrick were built in imitation of the strong stone watch towers of Syria. The basis of this slow evolution has been established by archaeology in the Wadi Natrun and elsewhere.

Pacomius or Pakhome was an old soldier, a Christian convert and the disciple of an old hermit called Palamon. In about 320 AD he established his first monastery at Tabennisi in Upper Egypt. He ruled his monks with exact regulations and a code of discipline from the beginning. Their cells were round the fringes of a rectangle, and the needs of the individual came second to those of the community. Communities of men, and also of women, sprang up in imitation all over Upper and Middle Egypt. No doubt the closer community life was necessary for survival in those areas, though in Lower Egypt the two systems intermingled. Secular community organization may have been a model; there is a lot in common between a village and a monastery. The work done by the monks was supposed to be undistracting, to permit meditation; gardening was considered too exciting in the pioneer days, but the monks naturally went to help the local villagers in the harvest season. Deir el Abiad, the White Monastery at Sohag, is where Shenute, of whom we shall have more to say, was abbot in the last quarter of the fourth century. The tradition of Pacomius continued without much alteration for hundreds of years.

In Anthony's tradition, of which a number of examples have been excavated, after the tomb came the church, and after the church the common refectory, not necessarily in use every day. By the middle of the fifth century the conditions of life had deteriorated and towers of refuge began to appear, at least in the bigger communities. The evolution from this to compact, walled monasteries was slow, and the hermits were obviously reluctant to give up independence. The limited evidence of sites that have been excavated suggests that in early days the cells of anchorites with disciples were on a grander scale than one might imagine. Even at their last stages, some of the semi-scattered, semi-centralized communities did not fortify their walls. Others did so at any time between the fifth century and the seventh. Local conditions varied greatly, as one might expect. In the tradition of Pacomius, the monks lived behind high walls from the beginning.

We know the work the monks did mostly from literature, though some primitive machinery and some tools have been excavated. Weaving of rushes and palm-leaves into mats and baskets was a staple. One could do that alone. But as the communities increased, so did the variety of specializations. We hear of fifteen tailors, seven smiths, fifteen dyers, four carpenters and twelve camel-drivers, all in one Egyptian monastery. They had writing places, tanneries and bakeries. Everyone tried to learn bits of the Bible by heart. The men buried the women. After the night of lamentation, a boat would cross the Nile bearing monks with palm and olive in their hands; they would carry away the dead nun for burial, chanting their psalms. Some great men were buried in churches or old temples, with a name scrawled on the wall. It was in the process of her burial that St Hilaria was discovered to have lived most of her life impersonating a man, as a hermit among hermits. Some pathetic attempts were made to embalm the dead, with juniper berries and sprinklings of salt. Only at the last moment of our record, when the outlying cells had been abandoned, did monks begin to be buried inside their enclosing walls.

Pillars

St Symeon Stylites got his name because he lived for the final forty years of his life, in the fifth century AD, on top of a tall pillar at Antioch. The oddest aspect of his curious fact is that he had numerous disciples. He chose his perching place by trial and error, and at first, not unnaturally, assumed that it would not be widely imitated. His earlier companions and his first disciples were monks who lived on the ground. His pillar was meant to be simply a surprising form of hermitage. No doubt he was a gifted climber. Lucian in his book *On the Syrian goddess*, which he wrote in the days of paganism, had

already recorded the method of climbing up a tall stone represen-
tation of a phallus in order to spend seven days there, "in the way
that palm-trees are climbed in Arabia". The climb happened once
a year, the climber made himself a comfortable nest, and he prayed
for those who brought offerings. It was a ritual, in fact. Symeon's
climb was not.

There is no doubt that he became world famous, and although he
was imitated at first only in Syria, Palestine and Mesopotamia, his
personal disciple Daniel carried Stylitism to the shores of the
Bosphorus. It spread to Georgia, Thrace, Macedonia and Greece,
and even in the end to Egypt, which at first had been disapproving,
having a traditional prejudice that hermits should live in deserts.
The life of Symeon was translated even into Latin, and he exchanged
messages with St Genevieve. She called him "a great despiser of
the world", which is an understatement. The only recorded attempt
to imitate him in the West was unsuccessful. Gregory of Tours met
a Lombard deacon called Wulflaic at what is now Carignan in the
Ardennes in AD 585, and put his story into *Historia Francorum*. The
poor man got himself put on top of a pillar at the old temple of
Diana. (It was hard to find a good tall pillar; the same difficulty
emerges from several stories.) Wulflaic lost his toenails in his first
winter and his beard was stiff with icicles. He did achieve one thing;
he preached such a rousing sermon that the local people smashed
Diana's statue. But then some passing bishops made Wulflaic come
down, and one of them broke up his pillar behind his back.

Still, there were so many stylites by the seventh century that they
were treated as a special order of religion. We hear of "monks,
hermits and stylites". In a national crisis "let them emerge from
their cells and descend from their columns". It was forbidden for
any woman to go near certain kinds of solitaries, stylites included,
on pain of five years' penance. They were perhaps not fully dressed.
One imagines them like those melancholy brooding storks that used
to nest on the roofs of Turkish houses, only less sociable. It was
enacted that in case of barbarian invasion a stylite could come down,
but when the barbarians went away again, as in the seventh century

45

it was assumed they would, then the stylite had to resume his perching place. Some of the later ones had tiny hermitage chapels; one can still see the remains of one on top of one of the mighty columns of Olympian Zeus at Athens. A twelfth-century manuscript records a special liturgy "for the day of a stylite climbing onto a pillar".

At this point one must wonder what the social role of a stylite was, or was thought to be. Why did it seem to anyone a desirable way of life? Why did the people like to see their stylite outlined against the sky? Several answers are possible. To pray among the ruins of paganism, which were haunted by devils, was an old tendency, and to crow on a column at sunrise has an obvious attraction. The call to prayer from a minaret offers some analogy. The stylite himself wanted prayer and penance, but it is hard to deny what early critics of the movement pointed out, that on the top of a column one makes an exhibition of oneself. The stylites surely bore witness deliberately against the values of the world. The element of paradox and their inescapable visibility strongly emphasized their message. But from the people's point of view their prayers were specially useful, they were prophets, and they had power over the weather. Is that because columns were often hit by lightning, or just because they stood so high?

This question emerges from the enchanting life of the stylite Daniel. He was born near Samosata, as Lucian was. He entered a monastery at twelve, but he still nourished two ambitions: to see the Holy Places, and to see Symeon on top of his pillar. The Holy Places were unsafe, so a vision told him to try Constantinople, the Second Jerusalem. He got as far as Antioch with a conference of archimandrites. These officials took a poor view of Symeon at first, but the sight of him converted them. Symeon had a ladder sent for, but no one dared to climb it except young Daniel, who got the old man's blessing. Symeon sounds in the Lives of him a rather cheery sage. He is recorded as yelling down "Welcome man of God" to visitors, in the modern Greek form *Kalos erthes*.

Later in time, Daniel made his way towards Constantinople,

propelled by visions and resisted by devils. An official called Mark the Silentiary offered to get him a pillar, and sent workmen to put it up. They then found a balustrade for the top, but at night for fear of disapproval in the neighbourhood. A landowner called Gelanius, among whose vines this column was planted, arrived to protest. Then a sudden storm of hail ruined his entire vintage, and this miracle converted him. He offered Daniel a bigger and better column, and provided it. Daniel became a feared and respected prophet. He foretold the great fire of Constantinople of 465 the spring before it happened. It is fascinating to observe what was expected of holy men.

As for the discomfort, human beings have from time to time perched in other places just as odd. The top of a substantial column is the size of a cell. There the stylite stood, as one of the Lives puts it, "snowed on, rained on, and sun-shrivelled, and many came out unto him". Gregory Nazianzen, who I think is my least favourite poet in the Greek language, notices in his poem to Helladius a solitary who stood for years on end. If one were going to be a hermit at all, the top of a column would not be the worst possible place, except somewhere like the Ardennes. It clearly made the stylites feel distinguished and socially useful: they seem to be a Syrian and essentially an urban phenomenon.

The Hermit and the State

Hermits who withdrew from the world were not typical of the normal poor whose lives they parodied. The fact that they defined themselves against the world as its opposite meant that they were defined against the poor also. And yet Christ expects an identification with the poor. The word lowly (Greek *tapeinos*) is first recorded as a personal name in the Jewish community of Nahal Seelim about AD 130; it later became popular among Christians. In later days, monasteries defined themselves as great institutions; they might employ or help the poor, but they could not be identified with the peasantry, which had no such institutional weight. Even from the beginning, monks were an elite.

All the same, one might expect more fellow-feeling with the peasants than one in fact finds. Shenute, whose name is spelt in many ways and Latinized as Sinuthius, makes an interesting exception. He was abbot of the White Monastery at Atripe in the Upper Egyptian desert, where he is said to have lived eighty years, from the eighties of the fourth century to about AD 466. He died at well over a hundred. This formidable old man, who was a peasant by birth, wrote in Coptic an open letter to a rich local pagan called Saturnus. It contains a vigorous attack on upper-class paganism and a defence of the looting of temples and grand private houses by the peasants, because the houses are defiled by idols, by magic papers and potions, and by luxurious baths, built by the sweat of peasants and maintained by their sweat. Shenute is particularly vehement about baths.

This is as good a place as any to deal with the problem of insanitary sanctity. It goes without saying that it was not as shocking to the late antique Levant as it was to Gibbon, and is to us. The hermits and early monks in the Egyptian desert cleaned themselves by rolling in the sand, in the same way that certain marbles were polished. The method sounds effective, and by no means unpleasant. It can scarcely have been invented by hermits. When Shenute complains about the levies and the forced labour that went to maintain Roman baths in Upper Egypt, he has a point. He is one voice among very many in the voluminous recorded complaints of the Egyptian poor. But the filth of certain hermits was a self-punishment deliberately undertaken, it was a bravura of uncleanliness, a heroism of inhumanity. When Theodore of Sikyon came out of his cave after two years, he was a horrid sight; his body was skin and bone, covered in sores and worms, his hair was matted and horrifying, and no one could come near him because he stank so badly. He sounds as if he had gangrene. He was a parody of leprosy, a romantic extreme of self-inflicted suffering.

As Christianity colonized the heart of the official world, and in the end took over that world, romantic extremes withdrew to its margins. That is where strange cults, unworldly prophets and new revelations have always flourished. It was sectaries and heretics on the whole who maintained a pure-minded view of poverty, and as late as the Reformation it has always been disturbed and afflicted areas that were ripe for a new sect: ripe, that is, for rejection of the central authority. The fourth-century fathers of the Church diminished and blunted the Gospel. They would choose to comment on Matthew 19:21, "If you wish to be perfect, go, sell what you have, and give to the poor, and you shall have treasure in heaven", rather than on Luke 12:33, where the command is absolute with no "If you wish . . ." The world had to go on, and one of its institutions was property. That is why Augustine, if it was he, first elaborated the distinction between a precept and a counsel of perfection. Christianity had become an official institution, and many sad consequences followed. When the Bishop of Rome became the Roman magistrate, he began to employ torture, according to the traditions of the court.

The importance of this double thinking for the monastic movement is that from the fourth century onwards, "If you wish to be perfect" was taken to mean "If you want to be a monk". The existence of monasteries, which preserved in a fossilized state the purity and personal poverty of the desert, was somehow thought to discharge all the most inconvenient commands of the Gospel. The catechumens or aspirant Christians of the early Church, who might not be baptized and undertake full Christian obligations until their death-beds, had arisen in imitation of aspirant Jews called God-fearers. But now true and full Christianity could no longer be easily tested by martyrdom and must be tested in monasteries. There is a sense in which ordinary members of the Church have been treated only as aspirant Christians ever since, because monasteries have been defined against normal Christianity.

One must remember that the famous Cappadocian fathers of the Church were well-educated men, and members of an upper class. If they chose to set up a monastery, it could be on their estate. Basil chose a natural paradise. The early fifth-century tract on riches attributed to the heretic Pelagius is absolute for poverty. But St Gregory Nazianzen advises in smooth verses that if one does not choose to give away everything, one may give most, or "with what's superfluous use piety". Augustine explains that the story of Dives and Lazarus is not intended against the rich. After all, he says, Lazarus went to the bosom of Abraham, and Abraham was a rich man. The poor, says Gregory of Nyssa, must not demand even what they need for subsistence, as if it were a right. They must ask politely.

A monastery therefore becomes an artificial world within which one may practise poverty and humility, though the world itself, the monastery itself, is not poor. The paradoxes and tensions have been set up from which monasticism will suffer ever afterwards. It may be that the Gospel cannot be institutionalized, and yet it can certainly flourish within a monastery, as we shall see.

Cassian and Benedict

The *Rule* of St Benedict is a strange compilation of severities and sermons, tailing off into a catalogue of practical regulations, rather as Hesiod's *Works and Days* wander off from their impressive and ornamental beginnings into surprising bits of advice, such as never to piss against the rising sun. But Benedict's *Rule* is resonant and haunting. It is impossible to read it without being greatly moved by its perfect sobriety and seriousness. It has indeed inspired the life of monasteries for nearly fifteen centuries, and all the later rules and wisdoms of the monks have echoed it. Even the rules of the Jesuits are loosely based on it.

The accepted authority in the fifth century AD was Cassian, an Egyptian monk of dramatic severity, who moved to Marseille about AD 400. He wrote a book about monastic discipline for the monks of Apt, about forty miles away, and a series of Conferences, full of pungent spiritual doctrines and unlikely anecdotes about the Egyptian desert fathers. I have always found him a depressing teacher, but his influence remained unabated for a very long time. The moral handbook used by Jesuit novices was impregnated with it. I cannot help wondering how much of this influence was because of his memorable anecdotes. Even his rule has a grimmer ring to it than Benedict's. "If any monk desire to enter into discipline . . ." is an uncompromising opening. It says something for early Christian Europe that Benedict's rule superseded his.

Soon after AD 500 someone in southern Italy wrote what is called the *Rule of the Master*. This is a disorganized but not an unimpressive document. It gives the abbot Roman supremacy over his household as long as he lives, and lays down more or less the monastic conditions that Benedict must have inherited. It contains the pleasing provision that the abbot has a right to make a monk blow his nose in a manner likely to give least offence to the attendant angels. If this sounds bizarre about the angels, one should consider that when a seventeenth-century Jesuit got permission to join the Christian slaves at Istanbul and minister to them in the prison where they spent their nights, the Islamic clergy had him forbidden to ring his little church bell because it disturbed the angels of God, resting at night from their labours on the domes of the mosques.

Benedict wrote his *Rule* some thirty years later at Monte Cassino. His magnificent opening chapters are a shortened, adapted version of the *Rule of the Master*. The monastery was essentially a school to teach the service of God, and like a school it was to be very serious without being unnecessarily harsh. A great deal flows from this, and there is a sense in which Benedict rather than Julius Caesar is the founding father of our Europe. The oldest manuscript of Benedict's *Rule* to survive is in the Bodleian Library at Oxford; it was written in England in the eighth century, in one of the northern monasteries that had close contact with Rome.

St Benet Biscop, for example, who founded Jarrow and Monk-wearmouth, was in Rome during the sale of the great library of Cassiodorus, and brought home a magnificent collection of books. He took the name Benedict at Lérins, where he first became a monk, and although the rules he left to his abbeys included customs and regulations of all the seventeen monasteries he had visited, it was based on Benedict's rule. The Oxford manuscript was copied from one that he brought home, or Wilfred brought home, to England. Its magnificent lettering derives equally from Rome; St Benet Biscop brought home the head cantor of St Peter's, who taught the Roman script and the Roman ritual and music.

It has been suggested that although the Oxford manuscript is the oldest we have of the *Rule*, the ninth-century Sankt Gallen manuscript (Sangallensis) gives a truer version, being written in worse dog-Latin. The theory is that the English version has been polished up by a better Latinist. Nothing is fiercer than a *querelle de moines*, and I have no wish to stir one up, but I remain unconvinced by this argument. Benedict's Latin has a luminous quality that suggests he needed no correction, and the eccentricities of the Sangallensis do not appear to belong to the sixth century, rather the ninth. The very first word, Ausculta, appears in the Sangallensis as Obsculta, not a vernacular or dialect form, but surely a solecism. It has no recorded parallel except in one obscure and obscene graffito at Pompeii. This opinion is of course conjectural, but by raising all these details I hope to offer insights into monastic history.

Imagine a parchment book of about folio size, worn smooth and smeared dark with use on its first and last pages. It was read in chapter and learnt by heart. First letters of chapters are coloured in a pinkish red, and drawn with austere fantasy as if they were made of twisted paper. It begins, "Hear O my son the instructions of the master and attend in thy heart, and freely accept the moral teaching of a dutiful father and effectively fulfil it, that by the labour of obedience thou mayest return to him from whom by disobedient sloth thou hadst drawn away. To thee therefore my speech is now directed . . ."

After the opening sermon, which with no loss of austerity contrives to convey warmth and a personal voice, the rule deals with the qualities an abbot should have (later on it deals with the abbot's table as well), the duty of taking advice from the brethren on serious matters, the nature of good works, obedience, silence, and the attainment of humility in its degrees, which is a rather full little treatise. Benedict emerges as practical, tranquil, and kindly. He understood personal humility: earlier abbots had no duty to take anyone's advice. There is no drama about anything. His word for silence is "taciturnitas", which means quiet or speechless, a quality attributed by Horace to a river and the stars. It means habitual wordlessness and not speaking more than necessary, not the dead silent life of the Trappists of more recent times. This little chapter begins, "Let us do as the prophet said, 'I have said, I will set a guard on my ways that I may not offend by my tongue.'" The one on humility begins, "Divine scripture cries out to us my brethren . . ." After these chapters we come to more precise arrangements: On the divine offices at night.

The austerest thing about Benedict's rule is its apparent monotony, but in practice that would be mitigated by the slow, vast changes of the seasons and of the liturgy. It cannot be understood except as an invitation to the spirit; its purpose is the contemplation of God. Later theologians have made so many distinctions about mysticism as to befog this issue. Nature and spirit overlap, and ascetic and contemplative life are not distinct in the ideal examples of monks. Benedict does permit hermits, but they will only be monks who by virtue have outgrown their breeding-ground in the monastery and need a more absolute monotony and silence. Without this ideal, Benedict's rule is unintelligible.

Benedict reduces penances, and the same tendency is to be seen in other contemporary rules for monks, in Gaul for example. It was in the religious spirit of the age. The regime of work and vigil he outlines will have been tough enough, since by no means all the early monks were hard-footed peasants. Benedict abolishes fasting in summer, when work is hard and food more abundant, in the monastery as in the village fields. The fact that his monks are allowed to do field work is another change: his monks are no longer quite such an undistracted elite, and they are poor. Several of the grimmer features of life are "because of their poverty and need". In fact they are very like poor villagers. They will not be able to buy wine because they will not be able to afford it. On this implicit interdependence with the spirit of the age and the economy of the village much that is otherwise puzzling in the history of monasteries will depend.

Benedict's regulations of liturgy are as detailed as Constantine Porphyrogenitus on the ceremonies of Byzantium, and in the Oxford manuscript the marginal notes here are denser than usual. ". . . and all being seated in stalls let there be read on the lectern three readings by the brethren taking turns . . .", and so on. But the monastic oratory is foreseen to be simple and by no means grand. The grandeur of English abbeys under the Anglo-Saxons owes more to a Roman influence than to Benedict. Elsewhere in Europe it became normal under Norman patronage. By the eleventh century, even the manuscripts produced by monks at Winchester, at Reichenau and many other abbeys were finer than the work of the Stoudion, the great monastery of Byzantium, and no less rich. The Bodleian manuscript of the *Rule* of Benedict belongs to an austerer age.

The best learned commentary on the *Rule* is in French, in seven small volumes, by Dom Adalbert de Vogué and Dom Jean Neufville (1972–7). It is with diffidence and at my peril that I have differed from them about the precedence of the text in the Bodleian manuscript.

Gregory

The spirit like the wind blows where it chooses. But it is wrong to
think of monasteries as the simple result of a spiritual need or the
movement of an age. In Western Europe they were deliberately
fostered by the Papacy, and in the East by the Byzantine Emperors.
They were instruments of policy, and conscious centres of missionary activity and Christian learning, and they were agents of reform,
being themselves constantly reformed. The unmarried clergy of
the West were the result of papal and monastic pressure, and it is
not surprising that priestly celibacy took a long time to impose.
One cannot avoid the thought that it was the fox who lost his brush
who persuaded the other foxes to cut off theirs. Damasus the Pope
who was Jerome's patron was the son of a priest, and no one seemed
to mind; his mother is buried beside him. But the celibacy of the
monasteries slowly extended like an ice age to cover the ordinary
clergy. The offices chanted by monks were made the daily, obliga-
tory reading of every Western priest. To this day if the Vatican
releases a priest it is customary to let him choose release from celibacy or release from the monastic prayers, but not both; that is
certainly how things were twenty years ago.

This disagreeable subject is interesting here because it is
intimately bound up with the papal patronage of the monastic
movement. The monks were meant to make everyone more monk-
like; the battle for clerical celibacy was won in the West long ago
now, though rumbles of opposition are still to be heard. In the East
it was never won, because the Empire and not the Papacy ruled
there. Orthodox monks are celibate, of course, but priests can marry
before ordination and have families as they do in the Church of
England. All the same, the expression of monastic influence among

the Orthodox is that only monks, vowed to celibacy, can become bishops. The trouble with this system is that ambitious ecclesiastics who prefer power to sex make the worst bishops of all, and they do sometimes crop up. Nor is it decent that the married clergy should be lower and poorer, mere village priests, while the unmarried purr their way to promotion.

The difference between East and West comes to light in the life of Gregory the Great (AD 540–604), the wealthy son of a Roman senator and himself a state official, who in the end became Pope. In 573 he sold his possessions, gave alms, and founded seven monasteries, six in Sicily, and one in Rome which he joined himself. The Pope took him out of it and sent him as ambassador to Byzantium for six years. He retired to rule his Roman monastery as abbot, fired with the conviction that the hope of Christianity lay in monastic communities, and not in any connection with the Byzantine Empire. His intention was to lead a monastic expedition to England, since he admired the Anglo-Saxon slaves he encountered in the Roman slave-markets. But he was elected Pope and had to send someone else.

He was an able diplomat. He made peace with the invading Lombards, put his own governors into Italian towns, organized the extensive lands of the Church, and cold-shouldered the Byzantine authorities. He controlled his missions with a lucid prudence. His Latin writings transmitted the theological expertise of the greater Church fathers to the Western Church. He was a popular and in places an excellent writer, and his *Dialogues* contained plenty of miracles and romantic stories. He was the first pope to call himself the servant of the servants of God. He organized the liturgy. He wrote the first life of Benedict and promulgated Benedict's *Rule* for monks.

His own monastery did not follow that *Rule* precisely. The rules and customs of the monastic communities of the day were anthologies, and an abbot could pick and choose among rules. But Gregory reverenced Benedict and constantly shows his influence. The promotion of the *Rule* of Benedict to be the Western standard was the keystone of monastic reform for centuries, and the most important single factor in creating the monasteries of the West as they have been ever since. Gregory was a Benedictine in almost all but name, and it was through him, I think, that the monastic movement became a papal instrument. Direct Roman control of distant countries derives largely from him. So incidentally do the Papal States, and the separation of the Papacy from the Empire, and consequently from the Orthodox who were subject to that Empire. In an older Rome, Gregory would have risen very high indeed. His personal sanctity and monastic austerity made him all the more formidable.

He suffered from gout, which one must assume was inherited, and from gastritis, which he probably acquired as a monk. But he was an industrious and intelligent letter-writer, and ill health had no effect on his output. Manuscripts of the liturgy show him writing to the dictation of the Holy Spirit as a dove. In reality, he is likely to have done the dictating himself, perhaps to slaves as Augustine did. It is an irony that he is supposed to have liberated the Emperor Trajan from Hades. The Irish in the later Middle Ages maintained that he was descended from a long line of Irish kings.

The relevance of all this to the history of the monastic movement in Europe needs to be pondered. I think it is very great. Benedict is as practical as he is spiritual and profound. But the practicality and power of Gregory were also a decisive influence. The English Benedictine monks, in their practical and decent way, are still trying to make the world a little bit more monk-like: rather for better than worse, by contrast to what happens elsewhere. That is as much the legacy of Gregory as the legacy of Benedict.

England

Monasteries define themselves as white against black, against the world and against a rather conventional list of sins. And yet they are particularly pure reflections of each passing age. They are rock pools occasionally visited by the sea. That has at least been my own experience and that of various friends. And I can think of no more Victorian figure than Father Ignatius the monastic reviver, and no more essentially eighteenth-century figures than the French abbots who built those huge ornamental stone gateways, those deeply recessed libraries. The monastery tends to survive, because it is an institution and its economic foundation is sound, but it is constantly, slowly, being transformed, if only by the coming and going of generations. It may be shifted by an earthquake like the French Revolution or the English Reformation, but monasteries revived in France, altering about as much as the world altered, and English monks lived on abroad, though when they returned to England in the nineteenth century they turned out to be much like the rest of the minor gentry of their day. The present Archbishop of Westminster has lived most of his life as a monk, yet, if one may say so without offence, he differs in few obvious ways from the Archbishop of Canterbury.

It must be a myth then, or at least a gross simplification, to maintain that monasteries have or preserve a special culture of their own. In the early centuries of monasticism, they differed more widely from one another and from anything that followed than any monasteries differed after the spread of the Benedictine Rule. The Welsh, for example, appear to have favoured a system by which the abbot, as successor to the original missionary founder, ruled not a community of monks but a community of families. The church of

58

St Illtyd at Llantwit in Glamorganshire, which is now alas a suburb, is built on the site of Illtyd's cell and his sanctuary, and preserves many of the monuments of a monastic village. It was the Norman Conquest that brought the new style of life. Irish monks derived probably from Marmoutier and the influence of St Martin of Tours. From Ireland came Columban and the monks of Iona, and then Lismore and Lindisfarne, Gateshead and Whitby, where at one time an abbess ruled over men. In the south-west, it was Irish monks who founded Glastonbury, and probably Malmesbury. These swarming and irregular holy hordes were virtually annihilated by national and clerical organization, and even earlier by Roman and Benedictine regulations.

Yet in 650 only in Kent out of all England was Benedict's *Rule* followed. Augustine of Canterbury (596) was of course a monk of Gregory's foundation of St Andrew's on the Celian hill. After 650 the Roman and Benedictine influence spread through founders who had been to Italy, such as Wilfred and Benet Biscop, through the activities of Hadrian of Naples in southern England, and through the kings of Mercia, of Wessex, and of Northumbria. The important point about this historical crisis is that the new movement failed to last; its force was spent in a generation. Small houses became, as David Knowles put it, "family strongholds of those who hoped to attain immunity from taxation and public service by the nominal consecration of an estate to God". Some supported a priest or two with a lay abbot. Raiders burnt a number of them. In a hundred years nothing survived in Northumbria, in another fifty all over England the monasteries were laicized or derelict. Alfred had to send abroad for monks to live at Athelney, but even they failed to last. The only exception to this sad story is the uncertain case of St Augustine's, Canterbury.

The new wave began with Dunstan and the royal patronage that Dunstan enjoyed. A part of this renewal that has left a permanent mark on English provincial life seems to have been a purely English invention. It was the idea of turning bishoprics with their cathedrals into abbeys, with a monk for bishop, and a monastic community instead of the normal chapter of canons. Hence Winchester, Worcester, Sherborne and Canterbury, some of the most beautiful buildings in England. This system, which meant a severe extension of monastic influence into secular life, seems to have been invented by Abbot Ethelwold of Abingdon, who started as a monk of Glastonbury, but found the life there insufficiently austere for him. He became Bishop of Winchester.

It takes rather a short time for each new wave of reform to spend itself. While they last they are always internationally linked. They are like a practical appendix to the history of ideas, the ideas being themselves socially and historically determined. Oswald, for example, was a Danish monk from Fleury who became Bishop of Worcester under the new system, and then Archbishop of York. But his English monks belonged in principle to Fleury. By the end of the ninth century Dunstan and Ethelwold and Oswald were dead, but monasteries had begun to be permanent. In 1000 there were in all England above thirty houses of men and six or seven of women. These thirty include many that are now famous ruins. They all owned estates and some were already rich.

David Knowles rejoices in these communities "rooted in the soil of England and bound to the countryside and its population by innumerable ties of revenue, jurisdiction, and personal dependency". But the soul is a cricket that chirps as well among ruins. It is not clear that this kind of rootedness, which lines up the monks as haves against the have-nots, and appears to make their existence depend on a variety of social iniquities, including the near slavery of labourers, was really good for the monks, even if without it they might have perished. It is not surprising that two new waves, two visitations of the rock pools by the wider sea, followed: the organized Benedictine monastic reform imported by the Normans after 1066, and the breakaway movement of the Cistercians, who reached England in 1130.

Monastic historians tend to treat all these movements as reforms, wave after wave of renewal of the hunger for austerity and the search for God. The soul ebbs and flows, but has no history, it seems, and

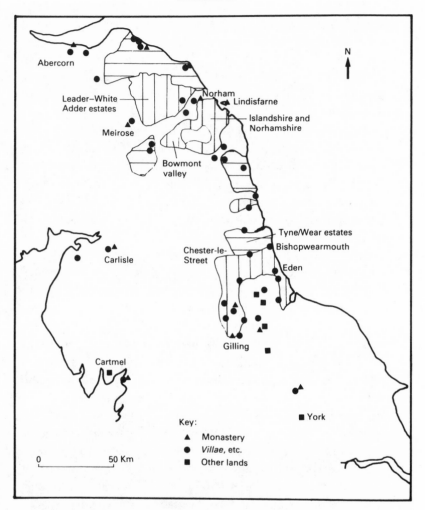

The rise of Church estates: land-holdings of the community of St Cuthbert by *c*. 720. From N. Higham, *The Northern Counties to* AD *1000* (Longman).

God certainly has none. But although the Christian Gospel underlies every Christian monastic enterprise, each one deserves to be
studied on its own, and they reveal great differences which have an
obvious relationship to secular history. David Knowles, the greatest

and most moving of all monastic historians, calls 1066 "the dawn of a day of great splendour", because of Norman control and Norman patronage in England. What happened is that the monasteries increased in power and wealth and influence as an important arm of the Norman feudal system. It is not maintained that they produced more saints than before, or better anything. At the same time the Conqueror moved cathedrals into fortified towns, and more of them were ruled by abbots and served by monks. This might tend to corrupt or relax the monks without improving the quality of bishops, but in fact historians seem to agree that it made little difference. Under the Normans the bishop of these places would be an ordinary cleric, and the monastic chapter was ruled by its prior.

I think David Knowles saw these events rather in terms of his own monastic experience. He certainly admired Anglo-Norman monasticism greatly. He belonged to a reform movement at Downside, and suffered for it. In his day it was unkindly said, though not by him, that the Downside and Ampleforth Benedictines were country gentlemen who were by way of being monks, while the Buckfast ones were monks who were by way of being country gentlemen. Downside and Ampleforth run large and successful public schools, and these upper-middle-class places had all but swallowed them. The reformed and austere Benedictine monasteries of France, which were devoted to liturgy and scholarship rather than to rugby football and little packs of beagles, seemed to young monks like David Knowles a more desirable model. He lost his battle at Downside and ended as a professor at Cambridge. The only monastery in England that lived the pattern of life he had wanted was Quarr on the Isle of Wight, a foreign foundation, as Buckfast also was.

The deep desire of monasteries is personal; it is the desire for God and the need for silence and for study and meditation. Bonaventure's book *The Journey of the Mind to God*, which in some ways reads like an appendix to Plato's Symposium, ends with the sentence, "Let us die then and enter into that darkness." That is the profound motive of monasticism, it is a kind of love. The sense that such a quest can be communal has often been disappointed. The individual soul may nest in a monastery for support as a bird nests in a tree, but the tree also has its life-cycle and its seasons of the year. With the Norman Benedictines the internal discipline and rigorous regularization of monasteries had reached their natural limit.

The Cistercian reform could go further only by breaking away to found new communities and a new authority. In England they increased swiftly for twenty years, and then slowly for another hundred, reaching their high-water mark in about 1250. The newly founded friars came to England between 1220 and 1230, increased swiftly for about fifty years, and touched high water by 1350. In the fourteenth century there were 1,000 and later 800 monastic houses in England. At this point the number of monks as a whole had already begun to decline.

In 1350 came the Black Death, which killed half the monks in England. By 1500 their numbers had climbed slowly back to about three-quarters of what they were in 1300. In the decline of the Middle Ages history was not on their side, and as the Renaissance dawned, the most inspiring changes in European life took place outside their walls. The monasteries could no longer contain the liveliest forces within them: Thomas More longed to be a Carthusian, and Luther and Erasmus were refugees from monasticism. So was Rabelais.

Athos

Athos, to use the ancient Greek name of the mountain, is called in modern Greek and even in Italian the Holy Mountain. Three substantial prongs of land like a trident stick out southwards from the coast of Thrace into the Aegean sea; Athos is the tip of the eastern prong. A craggy spine of land covered in woods climbs to a peak of marble 6,670 feet high that falls away steeply into the sea. This is the most sensational monastic site outside Tibet, and its community of monks is unique. It has been comparatively undisturbed for a thousand years, so that several different stages of monastic history have survived there and still flourish side by side, with diminishing but unexhausted vigour. Its origins are Byzantine, and it may be important that Athos is visible at sunset from the plains of Troy.

Athos is a wild place, a protected wilderness where only the monks live. The King of Kings, Xerxes, in 480 BC did not dare to send his fleet round those formidable promontories, though Herodotus records five cities on Mount Athos and some traces of them have been found. Xerxes preferred to cut a canal across the Thracian plain and leave the mountain to its solitude. It is an admirable place of refuge. The legends of its earliest monasteries are unreliable, like most Greek legends, but certainly in the ninth century it was haunted by hermits. They were almost certainly refugees from Imperial Byzantine persecution, at the time (726–842) when the worship of holy images was forbidden. The monastery of Stoudion at Constantinople was huge and powerful, but it was close under the eye of the emperors, and its history is part of Byzantine imperial history. Athos was more independent and wilder in spirit from the beginning. The first of its monasteries, Laura, was founded by Athanasius in 969. The entire mountain received an imperial constitution in 1045, by which no women, nothing female, not even a hen was permitted to live there. In 1060 Athos was granted independence as a monastic commonwealth.

The order of events is instructive. Laura is an old word for a group of aspiring solitaries living in a group guided by a father-figure, a guru or abbot. We have noticed such communities in Egypt. The foundation of community life in the monasteries of Athos is the written rule of St Basil, a well-tested document by the tenth century. But the impetus of the first monks on Athos was

Hesychasm or quietism, the solitary contemplation of God, induced by the mechanical repetition of simple phrases of prayer. Their inspiration came from Byzantine works of mystical speculation, particularly the *Heavenly Ladder*, by the Abbot of Sinai, and the *Spiritual Meadow* by John Moschos, a monk who became a hermit. Both were written in the sixth century. They were transmitted of course through Byzantium and the monastery of Stoudion, which flowered again in a reformed condition when the holy images were restored, and boasted a thousand monks. The old hermits of Athos were much wilder. One of them spent years in obedience to a verse of Psalm 49, moving about on all fours and grazing like a sheep. When Athanasius founded his Laura, an ascetic community that met in church three times in the year already existed. Such a community is called a *Skete*, and they still exist on the mountain.

The professional cultivation of solitary contemplation of the divine light in monastic communities led to impassioned metaphysics and furious controversy, so that although the mountain contained them all the individual monasteries tended to explode into fragments. The result is a system of forty differing monasteries in about 1400; about twenty survive. The latest was founded in the 1540s. In the fifteenth century monasteries of greater individual freedom and less oppressive regulation began to appear. In reaction against this relaxed discipline and against controversies, new reformed groups of ascetics came into being in the sixteenth century as offshoots of the big monasteries. There are now twelve of these. The parent monasteries often have a national flavour: a Russian, a Serbian, a Georgian and a Rumanian community. External events have had an influence. When the "Crusaders" took Constantinople in 1204 the monks on Athos suffered as badly as they had done from the Saracens.

They appealed to Pope Innocent III, who was at least sympathetic. When Salonika fell to the Turks in 1430, the monks swiftly submitted, and to that submission they owe their survival and the continuation of their privileges. A Turkish governor or inspector ruled from the little border town of Karyes, as a Greek official does today. But the monastic commonwealth still has its own elected council and president. The strength of the tendency to reform is reflected in the fact that the ascetic sub-communities are sometimes bigger than the parent monasteries. In 1911, Athos had three thousand monks and three or four thousand brothers. In 1981, after a sharp decline and a partial recovery, the population of the mountain was a little short of fifteen hundred.

Athos has its many ruins, but the landscape is inhabited. The big surviving monasteries are a strange mixture. Their beauty, when they are beautiful, has an autumnal fragility; it speaks to the outsider of history rather than eternity. The mingling of different styles of building is sometimes bizarre, and standards of religious observance and of behaviour differ just as much. One feels that every question about monastic life, from the sublime to the Gibbonian, is still alive on Mount Athos. The libraries and treasures of Athos have suffered the ravages of time and foreign rapacity. Parchments were used as wadding for cartridges by the Turks in the war of Greek independence, and for fishing bait since then, but Professor Lambros catalogued 6,618 manuscripts only a generation ago, and he knew of about 11,000. The frescoes on the walls go back at the best to the fifteenth and sixteenth centuries, but almost everything has been restored more recently. For better and for worse, the Holy Mountain is still very much alive. Even tourism has been kept more or less at bay. One must travel there on foot, and with special permission.

Athos is in some sense the heart of Orthodox Christianity. It is no longer rich, since the estates in Romania were lost in 1864, but it does possess outlying estates here and there. The essential development from hermits to grand monasteries, and so to relaxation and so to reform, each process taking more or less a hundred years, is a familiar story. So is the reflection of world history in monastic history. But the extraordinary thing about Athos is that the peninsula contains all these stages, and they have all survived together side by side. And unlike the Tibetan monks, let alone those of Western Europe, the monks on the Holy Mountain are more or less self-sufficient. They have never in any historical period battened on a peasant population. Their lives are bounded by their own monastic commonwealth.

The contemplation of God on the Holy Mountain was attacked with ferocity by Barlaam of Calabria as early as the fourteenth century. He accused the monks of spending their lives contemplating their navels. The monks were not slow to defend themselves, and Barlaam ended up accepting a bishopric from the Pope and teaching Greek to Petrarch. But the contemplatives claimed that they could see the light of God with their earthly eyes, a claim so simple as to be simple-minded, and the controversy with Barlaam swelled into a stormy and a raging argument. At Constantinople, the humanism that led to the Renaissance was already an influence. The quarrel rapidly became political and led to civil war, with both sides calling in the Turks with offers of free passage into Europe. The contemplative and mystical believers won, with results that have been permanent in Russian as well as Greek speculations about religion and about God, but the political results have also been permanent. The monks on the Holy Mountain went on contemplating God while the Byzantine world fell to pieces. They are an amazing survival.

Dominicans

Dominic Guzman was born in Castile in about 1170, some ten years before Francis of Assisi. His father was governor of the town and Dominic joined a mild religious community as a canon of Osma Cathedral. At thirty-one he was prior, and at thirty-four he met his first heretics at Toulouse, on his way to Denmark. He was greatly shocked. He founded a series of houses of nuns and associated houses of preachers, intended to convert the French heretics by silent example and by preaching. These are the origins of the Dominican

Order, and in the end of the largely Dominican instrument of the Spanish Inquisition. There is no doubt about Dominic's saintly kindness or his reforming zeal. He was a thoughtful and logical man, firm in his decisions and conscious of consequences, by no means such a lyrical or attractive creature as Francis. His Order began as monks with monastic superiors, but they were mobile and travelled light, and partly no doubt in imitation of the Franciscans, who were founded a little later, they became an order of friars organized in a similar way. These were the first orders of friars; they observed strict personal and communal poverty, at least in their early years.

Dominic's new Order was involved in tragedy from the beginning. In 1208 a papal legate was murdered, and church and state declared a crusade, an Islamic holy war, against the heretics of Languedoc. It is sad to report that the "crusade" was led by a Cistercian of Poblet, which to this day is the most beautiful monastery in Europe. Bernard of Clairvaulx had bequeathed his intolerance to his Order. Violence, massacre, torture and burning followed. The heretics seem to us to have been innocent people; they were massacred. Dominic's Order just went on praying and preaching. They took no physical part in the massacres, but they made, so far as I am aware, no protest. There is a parallel in their behaviour to what were called "New Christians", the Jews forcibly converted to Christianity in Spain who frequently abandoned their new faith and returned, secretly or even openly, to their old religion. They were abominably persecuted, without any protest from monks or priests of any kind. But the Order had its good aspect, and it must be said that the Dominicans reflected only the normal attitudes of society in a "spiritualized" way. Their unfortunate entanglement with heresy arose from their preaching and missionizing.

Dominic travelled in Italy, Spain, and France. He died in Bologna on his way to missionize Hungary. He left five Dominican provinces, sub-units of the Order each containing a number of houses, organized more or less by national divisions; there were already some Dominicans in England in his lifetime. Dominic himself three times refused bishoprics and wanted all the administrative responsibility in his Order given to lay brothers. But the Order became as powerful as it was widespread, and Dominicans rose to high office, including the Papacy. In Asia and later in the Americas they were a powerful missionary force, and it was perhaps the ineffectiveness of their preaching against European heretics that drove them to their more significant roles. They were unashamedly and professionally intellectuals, many of their houses being devoted to serious study of theology, philosophy in all its medieval branches, and natural philosophy. This was at the moment of the first rise of international universities, though at least Paris and Bologna already existed a hundred years before the height of early Dominican influence.

Dominic died in 1221; Albert the Great was fifteen years old and Thomas Aquinas was born in 1225. As usually seems to happen with the great monkish orders, their best years came early. Within a generation they had attracted and nurtured at least two men of undoubted genius, who were also great saints. In their writings they both combined monastic serenity with intellectual authority to a remarkable degree. They convey a sense of lucid and peaceful reason that cannot be turned from its course. I am speaking of course only of a style, the style being the man. It is not important to this argument that they were right or wrong, or even whether God exists or not. Some of their tranquillity was mystical, some of it, including possibly the mystical element, was inherited from Islam. It is remarkable and impressive, though it tends to disappear in translation. In the same generation the Franciscans produced Bonaventure, a rival of Thomas at the University of Paris, an exciting theologian but less of a rationalist. One of the very few jokes in the works of Thomas is what I take to be a mockery of Bonaventure's speculative theology, on the subject of the reason for some particular number of hierarchies of angels.

Albert the Great has some claim to be called the first medieval natural scientist, at least in the West. It is rather unfair to him that, because science has progressed whereas theology has stayed in the same place or merely disintegrated, Albert's works are now of less interest to us than those of Thomas. He was a Swabian nobleman who joined the Dominican order in Padua at the age of seventeen; Thomas was his pupil in Cologne. For two years in the sixties he was a bishop, but he was no good at it and resigned. His works on scientific matters fill thirty-eight volumes. They include astronomy, chemistry, geography and physiology. I hope I may find the occasion before I die to study at least his views on geography, which by the twelfth and thirteenth centuries had become a thrilling subject. Albert was an adapter of Aristotle and an opponent of the Arab Averroes, as Thomas was, though I have always suspected Averroes had the better of that long-range controversy, and I am sure neither of the friars was quite in command of Aristotle. No one bothered to canonize Albert until 1931, when the empirical and experimental character of his observations had come back into fashion even in the Roman Church.

I am able to speak personally about Thomas, because in my generation theological studies meant seven years of him. Intimate acquaintance with many of his works is a precious experience, but it is not worth seven years. Thomas was a theologian more than a philosopher, philosophy being to him a sub-branch which subtly flavoured all his procedures, even in his commentaries on Scripture. In my day he was taken more seriously by the philosophy professors, with whom we first encountered him, than he was by the theologians, who thought they had got ahead of him or behind him or wherever. But his works have a unity of style from end to end, and they are so clear that you can see from one end to another of his thoughts. It is therefore not surprising that his books were burnt in Oxford by an obscurantist Archbishop of Canterbury, and have been gnawed hollow with sub-distinctions ever since. I think that I owe my deep commitment to human reason to Thomas Aquinas, as others owe the same commitment to Voltaire or Diderot. You can trace his influence even in the mystical works of John of the Cross and the poetry of the Renaissance. His Latin poetry is on the level of Abelard's, who I think was a rather important influence on him.

Thomas was another nobleman: the early Dominicans were essentially an educated, middle- or upper-class order, if those distinctions have a meaning in the thirteenth century. As a boy he went to the monastery school of Monte Cassino until he was thirteen, then to the University of Naples until eighteen. That is where he took up with the Dominicans. His family were furious and locked him up in a castle at Rocca Secca, but at the age of nineteen he was a friar. He lived to be forty-nine, and his whole life was spent lecturing and studying. Not even that remarkable scholar John of Salisbury was a better or smoother, suppler writer in Latin. Thomas was a large, bald-headed, silent man, known as a student as the dumb ox. His master Albert rightly remarked that his bellowing would fill Europe one day. At the age of thirty-four he wrote an extraordinary and almost convincing defence of Christianity against Islam and the Jews and the heretics, based on pure reason. It was a remarkable enterprise, and one can see in it how the original purposes of Dominic could best flower. But it cannot be said to be typical of the later history of his Order. Thomas was or became a mystic, and is said to have despised his own theological works in the light of his knowledge of God at the end of his life. He is also said to have had teeth painlessly extracted by putting himself into a contemplative trance. He believed that music or a hot bath were permissible remedies for sadness in monastic life, an opinion he appears to have based on the life of Augustine.

There are more Dominican saints and worthies than I know the names of. My own favourite is Martin Porres, a lay brother whose lifework was comforting the slaves as they docked in America. He is also said to have raised a dead dog to life, which indicates a pleasant character. The Order was at its worst in Spain, where they became the watch-dogs and guard-dogs of an orthodoxy defined largely by themselves, and sniffers-out of everything unorthodox, from mystics to Jesuit theologians. In Rome they played a similar part, though without teeth, as lately as the present century. Teilhard de Chardin suffered from them, and so did numerous professors of Scripture. I was taught the rudiments of Hebrew by an old professor who remembered a time when every sentence in the account of creation in the Book of Genesis had to be taken literally, with the single exception that it might not have been an apple, it might have been a pomegranate. As late as the sixties, Catholic priests had to swear something called the Antimodernist oath before their ordination, which bound them among other details to reject socialism, and by a sub-clause to reject the opinion that Protestants expounded the Scriptures better than Catholics. It is probable that very few of them read through it.

The history of the Dominican Order, though they were monks of a kind, throws a gentle light by contrast on the quiet, unprogressive abbeys where theology never much flourished, where nobody missionized, and preaching was in an older, more nourishing tradition. Still, all the religious orders interacted, particularly as the Middle Ages drew to a close and more and more sub-varieties of monks and nuns were in competition. It was inevitable that there should be conflict. One of the early works of Thomas was a bold defence of the idea of a friar, as a legitimate extension of evangelical principles and of monastic tradition. One of Dominic's original intentions had been to shame the Cistercian preachers into a higher standard. The strength of the Benedictine abbeys and their sub-species was that they had in them the elements of survival and fertility. The new orders flared up and died or lost their edge and their attractiveness to the young. The abbeys outlived them. If they crumbled a little, they did so very slowly. I think this was because their purpose was private, inward, contemplative even, and their task was internal and liturgical and well defined. It is also true that their financial basis was solid and scarcely troubled the public. The intriguing friars of Italian Renaissance comedy, and even Shakespeare's rather sweeter friar in *Romeo and Juliet*, reflect a religious order with a higher profile than the Benedictines had.

The work of the Dominicans in modern times has been remarkable all the same. The rather mysterious group of artists that gathered around Eric Gill at Ditchling in Sussex, and later in Wales, including David Jones, an artist unparalleled since Blake, was under direct Dominican inspiration, and Dominicans took part in the revival of fine printing and of the liturgical arts in the twenties and thirties. It is perhaps even more to their credit that they have refrained from the more recent and disastrous movement that has left pseudo-modern churches on every bypass crying to heaven for vengeance. But the Dominicans themselves would probably place their principal modern contribution in the study of Scripture, and that has in fact been great, particularly in biblical archaeology, based on the Ecole Biblique in Jerusalem. A long session based on that institution is compulsory for all students of the Biblical Institute in Rome, which means for most Catholic professors of biblical studies.

Père de Vaux must have been one of the best loved as well as the most intellectually distinguished Dominicans of recent years. His works appeared with no less than four censors' signatures, saying *Nihil Obstat*, nothing against it, signed by two Dominican masters in theology, *Imprimi potest*, it can be printed, signed by the Vice-Master General of the Order, and *Imprimatur*, let it be printed, signed by the Vicar-General of the Archdiocese of Paris. I do not know what else vicars-general do. In spite of all this, Père de Vaux had a remarkable breadth and freedom of mind, and an unshakeable incision of reason. He was an admirable archaeologist, and a serious thinker about everything to do with biblical history, which has an importance, of course, whether one is a Christian or not. I never met him or worked under him, but I have often heard of him as a charming host and a powerful director of studies. It may be that now for the first time since the thirteenth century the reactionary position of the Church having been irreparably shaken, a Dominican can be compared with his great predecessors. Albert would have been fascinated by Père de Vaux's writings, and Thomas would have devoured them. His *Institutions de l'Ancien Testament* is a brilliant and fundamental textbook, but his specialized researches go a lot further. I feel particularly indebted to him for an article about why Jews were not allowed to eat pigs. The argument is archaeologically based and I think incontestable; it is also extremely surprising. I have written about this in a poem entitled "Pigs".

The first Dominicans arrived in England in an acceptably official way. They crossed the Channel with the Bishop of Winchester, who took them straight to the Archbishop of Canterbury. The first Franciscans came three years later, and in their first lodgings they had to huddle together for warmth like a pile of puppies. The Archbishop made the head of the Dominican commando preach him a trial sermon impromptu, and was so impressed with the result that the Dominicans were his best friends in a matter of minutes. They made immediately for Oxford by way of London, through the beech woods of the Chilterns; in those days High Wycombe was a forest track. By 1260 they had 36 English houses, and by 1272 they had 48, virtually all in cathedral cities and important towns. In the end they had 53; the Franciscans never had quite so many. But while the first Franciscans in England were shivering in their Canterbury room, Francis was receiving the stigmata in his hermitage on Mount Alverno. The histories of the two orders were similar in England in the next generation, when the Dominicans were closer to reforming bishops, and the Franciscans closer to the people. The Dominicans were household chaplains to great lords and confessors to kings: in fact they were very like what the Jesuits became when they were founded in the sixteenth century. No doubt that is why those two orders quarrelled so bitterly. But that is beyond our scope; the Jesuits were not monks while the Dominicans all but were.

I have chosen to follow the fortunes of the Dominican rather than the Franciscan Order because of the light they cast on many matters which were central to the Church, and which ought to be discussed somewhere in a book about monasteries. By going into detail about Dominicans I have inevitably removed them from the world context of monks as a human phenomenon, but I hope that readers will make their own comparisons and so restore that context for themselves. The Dominicans are closely bound up with European history. They are a reaction of those who made the monasteries to the changing conditions of Europe. This power of deliberate adaptation is a particularly European phenomenon; it is intellectual and depends on a relatively developed economy. There was no Europe in which Dominicans could have flourished in what used to be called the Dark Ages. History produced them, for better and for worse.

Suppression

It was not new in the sixteenth century that the monarchy should envy the wealth of the monasteries and dislike their privileges. The same thing had happened in China under the Tang. On a small scale it had long been true that monasteries had to be fortified against non-believers at least. A fine book of photographs could be produced of fortified monasteries, in Sussex, on the French coast, in Serbia fortified against the Turks, in Sinai against the Bedouin, who were paid a sort of Danegeld and acted as "protectors" of the monastery, and so on. One of the most beautiful, with exquisitely fine Byzantine buildings encircled by huge square towers, is Manasija in Yugoslavia. The founder of Arles had to move inside the defences within two or three years of his foundation. But the difference in England is that Henry VIII was a Christian prince. All the same, things are not simple.

The old relationship of patron and monk was quite clear. Whatever other advantages he might get from his monastery, direct or indirect, the patron expected to be prayed for. This is elegantly expressed on a monument at Godshill in the Isle of Wight, where the recumbent figure of the dead lord in splendid white marble has two Carthusians at their beads carved on the soles of his feet. He died in the fifteen-thirties, but the eccentricity of the design suggests that he may have designed his own tomb earlier. One can tell that the monks are Carthusians because they rest their heads on one hand, in the Carthusian manner of meditation. When Thomas

Cromwell made his will in 1529, he left money to four London friaries. I do not think there was great ill feeling against monks in the late Middle Ages, except in so far as they were landlords like any other landlord. There was much greater hatred of the wandering, begging monks called friars than of the monasteries. Chaucer was fined as a young man for beating a Franciscan in the Strand, no one knows quite on what provocation. Reform was a public concern, and it was clear to such orthodox figures as Thomas More, who had himself felt the stirrings of a Carthusian vocation, that many monastic houses needed to be reformed. The composer John Taverner whom Wolsey tolerated as a harmless musician left his work as choirmaster of what is now Christ Church Cathedral to be Cromwell's agent in the suppression of monasteries. He abandoned church music and died soon afterwards. He was a Lincolnshire man and lies buried at Boston Stump. Meanwhile the monks went on building down to the last minute of the last hour, as no doubt the human race will do.

The first foundations to fall were the English sub-houses of foreign mother-houses. They were suppressed or taken over by English abbots in the fourteenth and the early fifteenth century. In the later fifteenth century it became normal for patrons like Bishop Waynflete of Winchester to acquire and suppress decayed religious houses for the endowment of Oxford or Cambridge colleges. The universities had been rejected by the monasteries until too late; now they began to eat them. It is also to be noted that almshouses for the aged poor and charity schools had begun to be founded, often together, long before the suppression of monasteries is supposed to have first made them necessary. The Bishop of Ely made Jesus College, Cambridge, out of a dying nunnery. Mottisfont Abbey, one of the most beautiful of country houses of its kind in our own lifetimes, was suppressed by Henry VII to endow his chapel at Windsor. St John Fisher, Bishop of Rochester, gave the lands of withered nunneries to St John's College, Cambridge, in 1524. Still, there is no doubt that a mood of national independence and royal avarice give this tendency new energy, though in France, in Spain and in Germany similar movements had no anti-papal colouring. Henry VIII's antiquary Leland makes it plain in the notes to his Latin topographic poem "Swansong" that Henry's action against monastic houses stands in the tradition of Henry V.

Wolsey obtained powers of jurisdiction over monasteries by 1524, and initial powers in 1518. He treated the monks with anger and disdain, but he was not interested enough to enforce his reforming statutes, and we have no record of their precise contents; he dealt with them as a politician with financial plans of his own. Between 1524 and 1525 he suppressed twenty-one foundations to endow and build what became Christ Church, Henry VIII's counterblast to the Collège de France. Only four of these had above seven monks in it, but taken together their wealth was great. His agents were ruthless and aggressive; one of them was Thomas Cromwell, an efficient but unscrupulous servant of the Crown, who took over on a grander scale under the King when Wolsey fell. His portrait by Holbein in the Frick Gallery in New York is full-blooded and to my mind terrifying. The royal instrument, which Henry and Cromwell prepared between them, was a series of Acts including that of Supremacy, which the monks must swear to observe, including a denial of the Pope's authority. The Act of Supremacy got its teeth from a Treason Act. By the end of 1535 nearly all monasteries had accepted the oath required of them. But in January 1534 a commission had already begun to investigate the wealth of every house.

The exceptions were the London Carthusians and a house of Bridgettines at Syon Abbey on the Thames, which was barely a hundred years old. Its nuns were well-born and the convent very wealthy. They were closely associated with the Carthusians, and their male counterparts had been fellows of colleges; they were solidly opposed to Henry's divorce and remarriage. The details of the behaviour of these nuns are unknown. One scarcely credible source reports that they were converted to Protestantism by the dark eyes and sweet words of Anne Boleyn as queen. Whatever else happened, Richard Reynolds, one of the greatest English theologians of the day and fellow of Corpus Christi, Cambridge, who had been a member of their house, went to the Tower, spoke boldly and as wittily as More at his trial, and was executed with the Carthusians. All the same, the female community continued to give trouble. They were dispersed and pensioned off in the end, and Syon was sold in the autumn of 1539. The Prior of the Carthusians in London itself was a gentleman by birth and education, but a profound, austere monk, probably under the influence of *The Cloud of Unknowing*, and awkwardly for the King and quite obviously, a saint. For a time the Carthusians were left in peace, because they were extremely well known and greatly respected.

When the commissioners of the oath arrived in 1534, the Prior replied that what the King did was no business of the Carthusians. He did in the end swear and persuade the others to swear an acceptance of the royal succession, but the rejection of papal authority that the Treasons Act imposed was too much for all of them. The Prior was frightened of the consequences for his younger monks if the Charterhouse should be suppressed. They prepared themselves for three days. On the first they all made general confessions of their sins, on the second they each asked pardon of all the others in turn for all offences, and on the third the Prior sang the Mass of the Holy Spirit asking for guidance. At the elevation of the host everyone present heard the rushing of a mighty wind or an unearthly harmony. The Mass had to be halted for several minutes. They were tried and found guilty, and executed in their habits by the King's orders, so that it hurt more. As they left the Tower Thomas More was watching them from his prison window.

The lesser monasteries were suppressed by law in 1536, when the visitation of monasteries of 1535–6 in the King's name was still unfinished, but some of the weaker houses had already surrendered themselves. At the first news of the act, even before it was passed, the air was thick, as David Knowles puts it, with wings making for the carrion. Lord Lisle wrote at once to Cromwell from Calais where he was governor, "beseeking you to help me to some old abbey in mine old days", and he was not the only one. Even the

Duke of Norfolk felt that "where others speak I must speak too". Mary, as Queen, was forced to promise at once that she had no intention of restoring monastic lands from the new owners. Many families did well out of the transactions and some flourish to this day. The fate of abbey buildings varied greatly, but most of them suffered gross dilapidation and looting.

The visitors drew up an appalling list of monastic abuses, a transcript of which is in the British Library. No doubt this document is wildly unreliable, like the report of a state commission under Stalin. It contains a startling quantity of solitary sex and homosexuality, particularly in the North where the visitors may have favoured this line of enquiry. There was also said to be plenty of fornication. If modern experience is any guide, stray cases of all these things would be bound to occur, but they would not be anything like so numerous. I certainly do not see how the visitors would find out about something solitary, unless it had been confessed to the other monks in chapter, which I am sure it would not be and would not be allowed to be. Other commissions of local gentry reported more favourably. We have these documents for about seventy houses, and very few indeed and very few individuals get bad reports in them. In cases where the official visitors and the local gentry overlap in one house for the same period, the disagreements are striking. The visitors accuse two nuns of bearing children, but one was seventy and one was forty-nine, and the commissioners give both a good name. It appears to me that the official visitors were coarse-minded liars.

The lesser houses, those with a dozen or fewer monks and nuns, went under by Act of Parliament. In the course of 1536 a rebellion broke out in virtually the whole of the North. Some priests, such as the Archdeacon of Richmond, who was later instrumental in founding the grammar school and almshouses at Kirkby Hill, opposed it, but others were seen in arms. One of its principal aims was a petition to save the monasteries. There was no mob murder and no bloodshed except in the separate rising in Lincolnshire. They threatened to burn Kirkstead Abbey down unless the monks agreed to join them, and next day the Cistercians of Kirkstead did join in, under their Bursar and Cellarer, who were mounted and armed with great axes. The Abbot pleaded infirmity. In general, the religious houses hung back, though not without exception. The Abbot of Jervaulx ran away and "tarried in a great crag" for four days. The Abbot of St Mary's, York, was made to lead a procession, but he dropped his cross and ran. But Sawley had recently been suppressed: the people restored it, and Sawley became a centre of resistance. Not unnaturally, but the King took it badly. He told Lord Derby to hang the Sawley monks on their own steeple if gallows were lacking.

In 1537, the King was still making new foundations, moving the Chertsey monks to Bisham and setting up a better convent at Stixwold in Lincolnshire, to pray for his soul and the Queen's. At the same time, a number of houses were surrendering themselves. When the official visitors claimed that some individual monks or nuns asked to be released from their vows, they may well have been telling the truth, and one can see why in the climate that prevailed an entire house might wish to be dissolved. The legal position was in dispute, but the fruit was falling. Lord Lisle's agent wrote to him in January 1538, "I pray Jesu send you shortly an abbey, with many good new years." In the course of the next two years, the greater monasteries and the cathedral priories surrendered one by one. One of the royal agents at this time was John London, a Winchester and New College man, sometime Warden of New College, who persecuted relics and Lutherans with equal ferocity, and died in prison in the end. He found two rival heads of St Ursula in one district, and "a chowbone of saynt Ethelmold" and swept the churches bare. Precious metal was sent up to London.

Superiors were given serious pensions because their position gave them great influence and their signatures were needed. The poor old Abbess of Godstow, who particularly hated the Warden of New College, got £50 through him while the Prioress got £4 and the nuns £3 each. The Abbess of Syon got £200, which was a lavish annuity reflected in her fine memorial brass at Denham; the Treasurer got £13 and the nuns £6 or £7. The Abbess of Amesbury refused, and when she did resign got nothing. The Abbot of St Albans refused too, but he was pensioned in the end. The new Bisham monks joined gleefully in the auction of church vestments, and auctioned their own cowls in the cloister. Some few Benedictine abbots were executed: Hugh Cook of Reading, Thomas Marshall of Colchester, and Richard Whiting of Glastonbury, the last on a charge of robbery of his own abbey church. His head was stuck on a spike over the abbey gateway. The monarchy proceeded to the suppression of the friars. Protestantism brought a married clergy, which in the course of time we have all come to respect. Six hundred years before, reforming zeal had turned the married clergy out of Winchester; now they were back.

Even so brief an account of the end of the old English monasteries is bound to be unbalanced, because of the degree of unjust and oppressive behaviour, and because of the tragedy which monastic ruins eerily symbolize. Yet if by an impossibility a free parliament of let us say intelligent and liberal time-travellers could have debated what was to be done, is it certain that we would all have voted for their survival? The main question is that of the utility of these institutions and of course the distribution of wealth. How much more had the monasteries to contribute intellectually or morally to English life at that time? The end of the Middle Ages brought the beginnings of a serious modern literature within one generation. Some old men in Shakespeare's first audiences remembered the monks. Literacy and individuality of mind arose from the wind of freedom that blew in the ruins of the Middle Ages. History became more serious when it ceased to be monastic. Energy that would have chanted in an abbey and meditated in a cloister went into other things. I do not want to exaggerate, and I am not certain of the answer to these questions. In France the monastic orders continued until the Revolution, but without great intellectual distinction perhaps, except in the study of their own history and that of the Church by methods which no monastery could have first engendered.

I find it fascinating that we have an account of the suppression of the English monasteries written in his own language by a Greek refugee from Corfu who fought for Henry VIII against Scotland and then France in the regiment of Thomas of Argos. He described much of Europe, in fact, having been a member of an embassy in the Imperial service, a fertile source of travel books little known today. His name was probably Andronicos, but he is known from a nineteenth-century English publication of a fragment of his book as Nicander Nucius. He seems to have been well disposed to the Reformation. He liked the purity of the interior of Hayia Sophia at Constantinople, whitewashed as effectively by the Turks as if they had been the Warden of New College. And he admired the King of England for dealing so firmly with the monks. He gives a speech of Henry to Parliament. I do not know where he got it. No one in England is known to have read him before his editor of 1841, though Montfaucon had heard of him, and the incomplete Oxford manuscript once belonged to Laud.

He is reliable but bizarre about most contemporary events, but when he got to England the monasteries were already suppressed; still, he does reflect what he was told. He thinks the kings of England showed great reverence to the Church and obedience to Rome, so that the Pope got plenty of money from them, "and their veneration of the clergy went so far that almost the greater part of the island was assigned to the clergy, and most of the revenues went to them. Hence all over the island one sees numerous monasteries and enormous churches, in cities and in the country alike. . . . They often domineered over the citizens and treated Kings with contempt." The abbots looked like grand nobles or princes, with their retinues of horses and mules. Nicander then tells the story of the murder of William Rufus by two monks and the poisoning of King John by a monk. These are not original stories, but so lively that they do not seem to come from a printed source. "Henry came to the throne, and being of an energetic and spirited character he put things on a better footing." We are told first of his marriage and the case for annulment. When only Paris among foreign universities supported him and the Pope refused him, he summoned what sounds like Parliament. Henry's speech is against papal pretensions. "He does not hold in his hands the keys of faith, nor can he open and close as he chooses, but all have partaken of grace and preaching has been disseminated . . . mankind has tasted the nectar of the knowledge of God." The King appeals against papal tyranny. "I will be therefore the defender and vindicator of our faith, and I shall oppose those that oppose it in word or deed."

"All but a certain few" then agree to abandon Rome. The churches, the monasteries, Ireland and the small islands accepted this. Henry produced a giant gold coin (medal?), "the weight of twenty-five gold pieces", inscribed in Hebrew, Greek and Latin, "Henry . . . Defender of the Faith, Supreme Head of the Church of England and Ireland". He was said to have done it by the advice of clever and learned Anne Boleyn. She then had sexual relations with her brother, by her mother's advice, so as to produce an heir for Henry. The King heard of this and wanted to see it for himself; he actually witnessed it. The three were publicly accused, Anne spoke up for her brother and mother, and "all wept". Henry had their heads cut off. Nicander carries on through the other wives. The important point about all this is that the monasteries are apparently dissolved in silence, like snow. And so, the King's marriages come first, and then the bad morals of the monks. So far, they are simply an instrument of Roman tyranny, and Henry threw them off. Princes and Pope are assumed to act from self-interest, but royal energy is to be respected as being rather rare in history. The tragic anecdote of Anne is new to me, though it must have existed as gossip, as a defence of Henry, who could not be cuckolded by her lovers, and who must have known as an eye-witness that she was guilty, before he executed his wife. A touch or two of this story recalls Shakespeare's Henry VIII. The abolition of monastic life is a tiny incident in a chronicle of intrigues. In Nicander's day the abbeys were still standing empty in the fields, and that is what he wants to explain.

He then speaks of the wickedness of the friars, particularly the Franciscans. He has a story about a silver cross of pretended antiquity, which the Franciscans claimed to discover by revelation and set up for pilgrimage. It nodded its head if you brought it enough money, and shook its head if not; your sins were forgiven or unforgiven accordingly. One can see that the Warden of New College would not have liked this cross. The friars were betrayed by the Dutchman who made the cross, tortured and executed. This tale is entirely fantastical, and so is the next, about an old woman used by monks as a kind of oracle; the King burns her alive. "And not only were they detected in these absurdities, but worse, they fell into the most shameful lewdness of whoring and fornication, natural and unnatural, so that there was no vice forbidden and strange among us with which they were not familiar." It is generally to be observed today that Greeks suspect sexual scandals cover a deeper political meaning, where the English normally suspect the opposite, but this was the age of innocence. Henry makes a long speech to Parliament against monastic hypocrisy and vice. This speech is hardly authentic, since the King quotes Homer twice, and dwells in gruesome detail on types of abortion. All monks and nuns are exiled. "And one might see the societies of monks and nuns, some fitting themselves to secular life, others taking wives in lawful marriage, and others again removing into Scotland or Flanders or France."

Nicander obviously approved of what was done. He says that only those who agreed to live virtuously were "abundantly pensioned off from the public treasury", though they had to give up monastic dress. "Moreover, they ordained that there should be buildings for the reception of strangers, and for the aged, and for the sick, and for maidens. And they appointed presbyters to serve the churches." As he passed towards London from Dover by way of Canterbury, he saw the relics of Thomas of Canterbury dragged through the streets in his coffin, publicly burned and the ashes disposed of by being fired from a cannon into the air. To this event I believe he is the only recorded witness.

Part 3

Various Examples in More Detail

Missionaries

It seems an odd idea at first sight that monks should be missionaries, yet from the age of Egyptian hermits before the persecution of Christianity ceased, they have continually emerged from their sanctuaries, Buddhists just as much as Benedictines. With the foundation of orders of friars by Francis of Assisi and Dominic in the thirteenth century, the special vocation of unleashed monks became an accepted way of life. The Dominicans took happily to the nickname *Domini canes*, hounds of God. Not all behaviour of these holy vagabonds has been equally inspiring to the laity. Even in holy India, some suspicion of mendicants exists. Hermits from the desert rioted murderously in Alexandria, and the disenchantment Chaucer expresses with the mendicants was very popularly felt. It seems to have been the unpopularity of friars that gave Henry VIII licence to take over the wealth of the more ancient foundations.

When Francis of Assisi told his disciples that simply to walk up and down a street without speaking was to preach an effective sermon, if one was a good and holy man walking as a monk walks, he made a point we can easily understand. The trouble starts when mendicants are institutionalized, when the dogs of God sniff out heretics and Jews, and when their preaching becomes clamorous. The Franciscans had played a part in the movement of peasants all over Europe who were disposed to resist oppression, to howl for the millennium and to throw aside authority: in fact in the break-up of medieval society. That movement at its best is embodied in Langland's *Piers Plowman*, where Christ is the good peasant, and in certain illuminated manuscripts of the Book of Revelation, where Christ is Francis and Christ is a peasant. Embittered controversies and venomous intrigues marked the theological quarrels of friars and choir-monks, particularly on the subject of religious poverty. They are really too appalling to record. The Spanish Inquisition was in the hands of Dominican friars, and was used among other things to attack other religious orders on theological grounds.

In my own lifetime I have known friars certain that pacifism was right when that came into fashion, and certain that extreme socialism was right a little later. There was no observable moment of uncertainty. Intemperate views vehemently held are perhaps inevitably the besetting sin of an order of preachers. And yet the extraordinary sweetness of Francis of Assisi can be felt to this day, and exists as an atmosphere in his Order, in both the Roman and the Anglican churches. Even the convent of Franciscan robbers that had to be shut down in Calabria ten years ago has its innocent aspect. The Dominicans have not utterly lost touch with Fra Angelico, or with Thomas Aquinas. But as a formula for life, it must be said that stable Benedictinism has been the most successful, and that all later adaptations run into danger by straying from the reclusive Rule of Benedict, the Jesuits among others.

The two most impressive expansions of missionary monks were the Buddhist expansion into China and beyond during the European Dark Ages, and the Irish and later English missionary expansion into Europe at the same time. The Irish missionaries were sometimes bishops who founded monasteries rather than monks who missionized, and their tradition goes back to Patrick's own habit in the early fifth century, though Patrick is not likely to have made his monastic communities as central to his scheme for Ireland as they in fact later became. The British fifth-century Bishop Ninian founded a missionary monastery at Whithorn in Pictish country, where the monuments of some monks survive. Finbar founded the Abbey of Cork and Boniface founded Fulda in the same spirit. The Burgundian Bishop Felix of Dunwich did the same at Soham, now a ruinous church on the brink of utter decay. But the Irish added to these normal missionary impulses the urge to accept "exile for Christ's sake".

Fintan of Rheinau was an escaped slave who ended up in a community of hermits on an island in the Rhine near Schaffhausen. St Fiacre was a misogynistic Irish gardener who lived as a hermit near Meaux. Welsh and Irish women travelled too. Ninnoc became an abbess in Brittany, and Breage and her brother were martyred in Cornwall. Sixth-century Ireland was thickly populated with monasteries, and it may be that independence as well as zeal drove some of the missionary abbots on their roads. The most interesting is Columban (543–615), who first set up in an old Roman fort at Annegray, then founded Luxeuil and then Bobbio. His life was adventurous and beset with troubles. The Pope on the whole supported the Irish, though he rechristened English St Willibrord more pronounceably as Clement. The worst disputes were over the date of Easter. The meaning of the whole, vast, complicated movement was that the barbarous but Christian outer fringes of Europe were being called in to Christianize the barbarian invaders of the Roman Empire. They were converts themselves and understood conversion. And in spite of distance and the date of Easter, they were loyal to the Pope.

The Symphony

(Regularis Concordia)

Monastic history has a European pattern, but it is essentially local history. The reform movements and the empires and influences of particular places and times did not last as long as one imagines, but the great individual religious houses did have a long, continuous life, of which their own monks were conscious. Monks take a vow of stability, of not flitting about from house to house. That has its exceptions, of course, and outside influences have often transformed the lives of communities.

Monastic reform hit England in the tenth century. St Dunstan was born near Glastonbury in AD 909, and through his life one catches insights into the monastery. It was called simply Regalis Insula, King's Island; it was a green Christmas pudding among the Somerset marshes, which began to be drained under the Anglo-Saxon kings. The monastery was loosely organized, and a place of pilgrimage for the Irish. It was probably one of those Gaelic foundations like Iona which had Irish origins, but it now belonged to the kings of Wessex. (Its famous connection with Arthur was a piece of fiction, belonging to the propaganda campaign for money-raising to rebuild Glastonbury after it burnt down in the later Middle Ages.) Dunstan was a kinsman of the royal house. He entered the monastic school at fourteen. His uncle and two of his kinsmen were bishops.

The reform, or rather regularization, of places like Glastonbury, to make them subject to clear and set rules, like the monasteries deriving from St Benedict, had already started. What Stubbs called "a strong tendency to pure Benedictinism" can be detected under Elphege the Bald. Monasteries did not all have the same rules, let alone customs, an incrustation of traditional practice that can modify the rules. They had, if anything, an anthology of bits and pieces of rules with a variety of origins. Dunstan was an organizer and a regularizer under the King, as Abbot of Glastonbury and Archbishop of Canterbury (at the same time).

He began his career as a courtier, but the other young men said he was a black magician, perhaps because he was bookish. He complained that they threw him down in very muddy water or watery mud, and trampled on him. It sounds like an early case of rugby football. Dunstan's Abbacy of Glastonbury was by royal appointment. He seems to have imposed the Rule of Benedict, more or less, but the earliest witness we have to English monastic life under the influence of European reform is the *Regularis Concordia*, the Symphony of Rules, which shows traces of the model of Cluny, some interesting traces of the German reform movement, through such houses as Verdun and Trèves, and plenty of local English eccentricity. But the basis of the Symphony is the *Rule of Benedict*. It was a rule for English monks agreed by Dunstan, Ethelwold and Oswald about the year 972.

The Symphony seems to have been used in several English monasteries, and the fragmentary Anglo-Saxon translation of it refers to Abbot or Abbess, where the Latin gives only Abbot. The differences from Benedict's Rule consist chiefly of encroachments on the time meant for private meditation and reading, by extra offices for All Saints and for the dead, and numerous and repeated prayers for the royal family. When one takes into account the fact that Anglo-Saxon kings liked to be buried in abbeys and that sainted royalty were strangely abundant, the influence of royal patronage becomes clearer. Kings knew what they wanted of monks. The prayers for the King may possibly have come from Germany, though in my own lifetime even the Roman liturgy for Holy Week still contained a prayer for the Holy Roman Emperor. Certainly as boys we sang a Latin response most lustily every Sunday, to music I think by Gounod: "God save George our King, and hear us on the day we call upon Thee."

The traditional Benedictine hour of private meditation between matins (now called lauds) and prime did not begin in England until after a wash, a change into day shoes, and some recited prayers. The five hours of Benedictine work were intruded on in the same way. In modern times in this country, school-teaching greatly interrupts the old, tranquil and pure Benedictine rule. The Symphony puts a great stress on entertaining the poor, both local and wandering, which is unique to England. It also provides for various drinks here and there in the week, for customary excuses, such as after cleaning, and a snack before serving or reading at lunch, and a drink after the Saturday Maundy. Three poor men had their feet washed every day, but on Saturdays the officials for the week, the servers at table, for example, washed the feet of the other monks. The ceremony was called *caritas*, and one had a drink afterwards. The Anglo-Saxon age is a long time ago, but there is something peculiarly English about the Symphony of Rules.

But it raises the question of servants. How much work were the monks supposed to get through? Were they a learned elite or did they have rough hands? And what about nuns? They are said to have gone unrecorded because they were illiterate, though there are plenty of references to them in the Lives of Saints. Was their work like other women's? Did the convent in Swaledale spin the wool of the Swaledale sheep? Convents, like monasteries, circulated a roll of the dead, asking in elaborate Latin form for prayers: each monastery or convent added its names. To judge from the Latin of Abelard's Héloïse, whose writing seems to have survived on one of these in the twelfth century, the normal standard of women's literacy was even then not as high as men's, even in a convent, yet the nuns knew Latin, or some of them did.

No one is in doubt about the fine arts, the carving of stone or the illumination of manuscripts or fine copying. The abbots of the Cluny reform corresponded in deliberately elaborate Latin that meant nothing much. Peter the Venerable had a particularly awful facility at this complacent game. But as for real work, we know that Ethelwold and his monks helped the builders at Abingdon and at Winchester, yet at Westbury on Trym, Oswald employed what they called *contemptibiles personae*, contemptible persons, to do the work, leaving the monks free for their equally mechanical task of praying for the King.

I am unable to resist adding one more rather English item in the Symphony of Rules. John Moore, in a book about the country round Tewkesbury after 1945 entitled *The Blue Field*, records the amazement of outsiders who saw working countrymen consuming their "snap" of thick slices of unbuttered bread with bacon. The Symphony of Rules agrees with Benedict that dinner is two cooked vegetable dishes, with apples or fresh young vegetables that need no cooking. Meat was given only to boys or the sick. But the Symphony, unlike its continental cousins, forbids the eating of *pinguetudo* at certain times and seasons. I do not see what this can mean, except bacon fat, or dripping, which was somehow not thought to count as meat. In the later Middle Ages there was a school of thought that believed the barnacle goose led such a queer life it must be a fish, and could therefore be eaten in Lent.

The Symphony is also apparently unique in not legislating for blood-letting, which was thought on the Continent to be necessary to monastic life. It allows shaving at mid-Lent and Easter, and a bath at Easter, "on Good Friday if necessary", which sounds as if shaving and bathing were regular practices at other times of the year (a relief when one comes to think of it) and forbidden only in Lent.

Ailred and Godric

In the long history of monasteries and religions, the twelfth century is an inspired moment. Ailred of Rievaulx, who lived then, was one of the most attractive of English saints, not only in his life by Walter Daniel, his charming friend and disciple, but in his own brilliant and friendly writings. He was never formally canonized as a saint except by his own Order, the Cistercians, but by normal human understanding Ailred was a saint and Rievaulx is a holy place. It is also one of the loveliest places in Yorkshire, and Ailred one of the most enchanting medieval writers. His best books were the Sermons on Isaiah and a fascinating treatise about friendship. He practised as he preached, but his greatest monument is the ruins of Rievaulx, much greater than the Rievaulx he left.

He was born in 1110, ripe for the full impact of the fresh Cistercian ideals. The Benedictine reform took its special Cistercian shape at Citeaux, near Dijon, in 1098, under an upper-class monk called Robert of Molesme, Alberic, a hermit from Collan near Chantillon-sur-Seine, and Stephen Harding, a penitent pilgrim from England. Citeaux did not flourish at once. It began as a splinter movement from Molesme in search of greater austerity of life, and it might not have lasted beyond the lifetimes of its early members, but in 1112, while Stephen still reigned as its third abbot, it attracted a group of thirty-two Burgundian noblemen, led by Bernard Sorrel, who was just twenty years older than Ailred. Bernard was very soon given a new monastery of his own at Clairvaux, and the extraordinary energies he unleashed have made him famous as Bernard of Clairvaux. Typically of Cistercian foundations, Clairvaux was in a wilderness, and he renamed it Vallis Clara or Fair Valley from Vallis Absintha, Bitter Valley.

Because they lived in wild country, which they domesticated, the Cistercians were associated with sheep pastures. The early Benedictines had always bought the cheap woven cloth in which they dressed; it was black, and they were called the Black Monks. The Cistercians worked in their own wildernesses and wore the wool of their own sheep, so they were called the White Monks, though at first it must have been a streaky, impure white, unlike the smooth and laundered impression they give now. In England, the wool trade was big business. Bolton Abbey kept as many sheep as the King of Knossos 2,500 years earlier, and the abbey was about the size of Knossos. Buildings in pure and massive stone and endless new foundations drew nearly every Cistercian monastery into debt before it was a hundred years old, and the English monastic wool trade was among the foundations of the Medici fortune in Florence. Monastic sheep financed the Renaissance, one might say. In several ways, in its best aspects, in their intellectual and mystical life, they pre-enacted it.

Bernard founded new communities in Yorkshire, Kent, Wales and Ireland, among other places, and when he died, in 1153, Clairvaux had 700 monks. He also inspired the Order of Knights Templar, which lapsed into spectacular decadence as one might expect, though older historians discount the spectacular degree of the decadence. Military aristocracy belongs to the not inconsiderable dark side of Bernard's moon. His involvement in papal and European politics brought his order papal support, and he flung himself into theological conflict of peculiar bitterness and into the promotion of a wicked, stupid and utterly disastrous Crusade. If ever a saint spent time in purgatory it must have been Bernard. He may be said to have invented the Christian European God of 1914.

But Rievaulx is an innocent offshoot, and not the only one. Fountains was a splinter movement from the Benedictines of York, in search of regularity and austerity, just as Citeaux had been from Molesme. Bernard sent his secretary William to be abbot. Ailred of Rievaulx was a priest's son from Hexham, and not I suppose a Norman. He was educated at Durham, and served in the household of King David of Scotland for four years in his twenties. David, his mother, his Anglo-Saxon father-in-law, and his son Henry's best friend Ailred, were all saints. This remarkable family record is not entirely due to the tendency of kingdoms to confer sanctity on royalty and its relics, which was certainly rampant. Sanctity, like other forms of human decency, is probably catching. Among the early Cistercians, it appears to have attained epidemic proportions.

Ailred's book about friendship recalls Prince Henry in an open and moving way. In 1134 Ailred went to Rievaulx as a monk; Rievaulx was then two years old. Henry died in a Scottish–English war. Eight years after joining his Order, Ailred went as a delegate to Rome over the disputed election of William Fitzherbert, Archbishop of York. William was a nobleman with royal connections; he was properly elected, but Bernard of Clairvaux and his Yorkshire commando wanted a Cistercian, and pursued William, who by the way is a canonized saint, with the most disgusting accusations and ruthless intrigues. In the end they had him deposed and the Abbot of Fountains appointed. William retired as a monk to Winchester, outlived his enemies, and died, reinstated at York, probably by poisoning. He was canonized in 1227 after a papal enquiry into his life, conducted by the then Abbots of Fountains and Clairvaux.

Ailred's role at Rome was probably quite innocent; anyway it was unsuccessful. He came home to be master of novices, perhaps for his personal experience of the monastic discipline of European communities, and then abbot at the age of thirty-three, first in Lincolnshire and then Abbot of Rievaulx, aged thirty-seven. He built up the Rievaulx community in his lifetime to 150 choir monks, and no less than 500 lay brethren, the manual labourers and servants who made the peace possible, and who probably physically built it. It is not quite certain who introduced these interestingly predominantly lay brethren to the Cistercian Order. Five hundred was a record for England. It may be that monastic life seemed a desirable alternative to life under the Norman aristocracy or the Scottish wars; most of the lay brethren will have been landless men, and some of them serfs.

Ailred was a sensitive and a gentle figure, unashamed of his ramifying affections. He was a good friend far beyond his cloister, and in the end a national influence, as so many enclosed religious have been down to the present day, both in the Roman and in the Anglican church. He did at times travel. In 1163 he preached in Westminster Abbey at the shrine of Edward the Confessor, two years canonized. The present shrine, which took twenty-five years to build, dates only from 1269, and had to be restored under Queen Mary in the sixteenth century, but the burial place was the same, and it was Ailred who installed the King's uncorrupted body in its first shrine as the relics of a saint. The King of England was a kinsman of Edward the Confessor through Margaret of Scotland. Ailred travelled also to the Cistercians of Melrose, which David founded, and to visit his friend Godric of Finchale, an old Anglo-Saxon hermit and yet another saint.

Godric was forty years older than Ailred, and his life had been eventful. He was born in Norfolk, became a pedlar in Lincolnshire, a swampy and gloomy place in those days, went to Rome as a pilgrim, went to sea in northern waters, rising to captain of his ship, and then went on a pilgrimage to Jerusalem. An unfortunate record exists of an English pirate of the same name and date ferrying Crusaders about in 1102. He got home through Compostela, worked for a time as a bailiff, then made two more European pilgrimages, one to Rome and one to St Gilles in Provence. He could clearly tell attractive tales of these holy wanderings; on his third visit to Rome, aged about thirty-five, he took his elderly mother; she had given birth to him about a year after Hastings.

In about 1105 he set up as a hermit. What inspired him was the thought of St Cuthbert on the Inner Farne, which Godric knew as a sailor. As a hermit, he drifted back to Jerusalem, where he lived with some other hermits in a desert and worked for a time in a hospital. When he got back to England he went to work as a pedlar again, to retire into a ruined hermitage near Whitby. Then he was a sexton at Durham, where he went to school with the choirboys. The Bishop of Durham settled him on his own land at Finchale. The Prior made him an honorary member of the monks. He lived with fearful austerity in endless repentance for various lecheries and dishonesties. The river nearly drowned him, the country must surely have come near to starving him, and Scottish soldiers killed his cow and beat him in search of his buried treasure. In winter he looked after the rabbits and field-mice. He lived to be a hundred and one.

Godric's life illuminates the background pressures of his generation in a way that Ailred's cannot. Not surprisingly, he was much visited in his old age. His kind of sanctity, his huge objectivity of mind, his inability to settle and his appalling appetite for punishment, suggest similar problems and qualities in other monks. He might have been a Cistercian recruit. He was extremely Anglo-Saxon. He found a living one way and another for a hundred and one years. He was a kind of holy tramp. Visitors said he talked little but listened a lot. For a time he had a cow, which no one would have mentioned if the Scots had not killed it. His sister Burchwen lived with him in his hermitage, with the cow, but in the end she died as a hospital sister at Durham. Strangest of all, though one might have guessed it, Godric was a poet and set his own English verse to music. It has survived. That is far more interesting than his letters from the Archbishop of Canterbury and the Pope. He was worth Ailred's visits. Godric died in the Durham hospital: Ailred lay painfully ill for a long time in a hut beside the Rievaulx infirmary, and died at fifty-seven when Godric was ninety-eight.

In the eye of God how much did they have in common? The

differences and the similarities are almost equally striking. The old wanderer and the courtly young monk were both headlong and austere enthusiasts. The restlessness of the holy tramp and the stable progression of the Cistercian are both blind, almost instinctive, drives. Behind them both looms the tragic history of their age in Britain. Interwoven with both their lives are many similar influences of the genius of place. Finchale is not very far from Rievaulx; it lies almost within sight of the North Riding. Godric chose his hermitage between Carlisle and Whitby, and Finchale and Rievaulx are midway. The two men were both in their ways very beautiful writers, Godric in a dying tradition that still haunts the origins of English poetry, Ailred in a fine, progressive, international Latin style which is now as dead as mutton. They differed in class and generation. Of the other names important in this tangle of lives, Bernard at least was a preacher of extraordinary eloquence and a mind capable of exciting and inspiring John Donne. He was also a mystic and a poet. I think I read as a novice that he composed his best mystical discourses in a kind of garden hut composed of flowering sweet peas. I suppose it cannot be true.

Holy Women

The lives of nuns and holy women in the Middle Ages give an impression of chance and the absence of an organized structure, compared to those of the men. They had no careers and no mechanical process of sanctification. Convents flower and wither more swiftly than monasteries. Nuns are still asking for a written rule centuries after Benedict; they are often governed by men. Their convents are founded by their fathers or their brothers, or they are members of royal families. The difference between someone's widowed mother setting up to live a religious old age with a few devoted friends not far from the monks, and the beginnings of a convent, is not obvious. And one must remember that the builder of a church became its owner, in England among the Anglo-Saxons as in Sweden, and in some sense much later in the case of monasteries. The fully bureaucratic regulation of nuns, with approved rules, male supervision, vows like legal contracts, and the rest of it is a rather recent phenomenon.

As late as the twelfth century the Benedictine mystic Hildegard was adopted and educated by an old lady hermit. The hermit, whose name was Jutta, became an abbess, and her adopted child succeeded her. Hildegard was a visionary; so probably was Jutta, but Hildegard wrote down her visions. They did not prevent her from shifting her nuns to a better site and founding and reforming other convents, and they encouraged her to write severe letters to a number of bishops, to the Pope, the Emperor Barbarossa, and the King of England. They all seem to have accepted her letters meekly enough. She was a poet as well, and wrote a play, a book of natural history, and a medical book. The medical book dealt with headaches, insanity, obsession, and the circulation of the blood. She also wrote some theological commentaries. She illustrated her own visionary book with pictures, which have survived and are extraordinary. The book is called *Scivias*, which is short for Knowing the ways of the Lord. She got into trouble for granting burial to the corpse of an excommunicated person, but she won her case. She lived to be nearly eighty. She was never properly canonized, Rome was terrified of the idea of such a woman, but she just sort of crept into the category of saints, and they admitted her in the end.

Etheldritha in the ninth century lived all her life as a prophesying hermit in the marshes of Croyland, because the king who wanted to marry her was murdered by her father. Ethelburga in the seventh century became an abbess in a more normal way. Her brother Earconwald was a rich and royal personage who was the Bishop of London, ruling Essex and Middlesex. He built a monastery at Chertsey where he lived, and another at Barking for his sister, though he died at Barking in the end, probably being looked after by the nuns. The two houses and the diocese all claimed his body, but he was buried at St Paul's. The old couch on which he used to be carried about was still doing miracles for years after his death, as Bede records, who was twenty when Earconwald died. Ethelburga is said to have employed a nun trained in France called Hildelith to instruct her in nunnish matters, and Hildelith was her successor as abbess. Bede was impressed by the stories about Ethelburga, and devoted several chapters to them. Most Anglo-Saxon nunneries were royal foundations, and most founders were sainted. The position of a dead royal person mourned and guarded by her women was very like that of a saint, and miracles seem to have been as common as raspberries.

Hilda, or more cheerfully and apparently correctly Hild, was the seventh-century Abbess of Whitby. She was royal by Northumbrian and by East Anglian blood, brought up in North Yorkshire where her parents lived as refugee royalty in the tiny British kingdom of Elmet. The ruins of Whitby, grand as they are, and later than her day, give some sense of the smallness of scale of these lives. The size of that abbey on the cliffs must once have seemed extraordinary, and the journey from Elmet dramatic. Rievaulx was still uninterrupted forest, and Rome as distant as the South Pole. When Hilda was a young girl, Edwin, the new King of Northumbria, who had just defeated and killed his predecessor at the battle of the river Idle, attempted to marry Ethelburga, princess of Kent, for dynastic and political reasons. She was Christian, and Paulinus came to York with her as chaplain and as a missionary bishop. He seems to have converted the pagan high priest. Some time later Edwin became a Christian, and many of his thanes followed him; Hilda, being of royal blood, was baptized with him. She was thirteen.

She was thirty-three, and one may assume unmarriageable, before she turned to monasticism. Her sister had gone abroad to be a nun, and she intended to do the same. It is not likely that they were rich. The monk Aidan of Iona, Abbot of Lindisfarne, an Irish-trained ascetic in the tradition of Marmoutier, Cassian's community, called her home and gave her an acre or so of land on the river Wear to build a monastery of her own. She moved soon afterwards to the Abbey of Hartlepool, in succession to the Abbess Heiu. There she organized the community on Irish lines, that is more or less on the lines of Marmoutier. She used the rule of Columbanus, an Irish abbot who died about the year of her birth. It was harsh, and stressed the need for physical self-punishment. Columbanus is supposed to have been sent into a monastery by an old lady hermit in Ireland, to whom he confessed the torments of sexuality. He was a good poet. Hilda's greatest success was to found, or perhaps refound, the Abbey of Whitby, with a men's and a women's wing over both of which she ruled. Similar double monasteries existed on the Continent. In the end she was queen of half the northern Church through her monastic pupils. More important, perhaps, it was Hilda who encouraged Caedmon, the first Christian poet in English.

Hilda was very much on the Irish and the Frankish side. She supported the Irish date of Easter, which split the British Church and got Columbanus into such trouble on the Continent, though at the Synod of Whitby, to which she was hostess, she accepted the decision to go over to the Roman date. She had been baptized with Edwin on Easter day, and as that must have been calculated by Paulinus it was presumably the Roman date for Easter. Her personal prestige grew, but under her successors Elfleda and Enfleda Whitby came closer to Rome. Enfleda was Queen of Northumbria, and vowed her daughter Elfleda to serve God in an abbey if King Oswiu should defeat Penda the pagan king of Mercia. Oswiu did so, and Elfleda was handed over to Hilda. Mother and daughter both ruled as abbesses; their lives are full of prophecies, wonders, royal influence and diplomatic skill. Whitby became the royal mausoleum of Northumbria. It was sacked by the Danes within a hundred years. It was refounded in 1100 as a monastery for men only.

In fact the first definite move to exclude women from the monastic life, or at least from the old double monasteries, was under the influence of Cluny, the first major Benedictine reform of the high

Middle Ages, in the tenth and eleventh centuries. The mark of Cluny was impressed on other houses in different ways, through a temporary abbot or a Cluniac admirer or the Cluny custom book. It was not a result of direct authority. The tendency to abolish the homelier system of double monasteries has probably more to do with the changing behaviour of European society, its silent conventions and presuppositions, than with a deliberate act of policy. It represents a decrease of tolerance and of the status of women, who were no longer a law to themselves; it represents an increase of male regimentation and a decrease in status of the old social links of blood and kinship. All the same there are exceptions. The Gilbertines flourished here and there from the twelfth century to the eighteenth, mostly in double houses of monks and canons. They were founded by the Englishman Gilbert of Sempringham and Bernard of Clairvaux helped him write their constitution.

The old English and Frankish position of women and its prestige for nuns is to be found in the tenth and eleventh centuries only in Germany, where nuns were often called canonesses. The Saxon royal family were specially fond of canonesses. Otto the Great died and was buried at Quedlinburg in 973, at the abbey of his daughter Matilde, and Otto the Second's daughter was abbess of the same place with three sub-houses. Otto the Great's granddaughter wrote to a distant cousin in England to know what had become of the family, since Otto's wife had been Edith the sister of Aethelstan. She was answered with a copy of the *Anglo-Saxon Chronicle* in Latin. It is all much like a parody of Europe a hundred years ago. The Christianization of Bohemia, as of much of Eastern Europe, was effected by missionary monks. The first two houses were a women's abbey founded by Princess Mlada-Maria, who was abbess, in Prague, and the men's abbey of Brevnov. By the eleventh century they had secular as well as religious importance.

Essen went in for aristocratic abbesses, so that their prestige and the consequent wealth of the abbey were huge. The treasure of Essen Cathedral, as it now is, derives from that age, and it is one of the most remarkable early medieval collections in Europe. The

convent was admired as much by bishops as by emperors; there is
no suggestion that it lacked spirituality. It simply reflected the social
relationships conventional at that time. Such things can ossify, of
course. There was a convent in Vienna, which I believe survived
the 1914 war, where no nun might enter the community if she had
less than eight quarterings. But it was not the convent that had
ossified, it was Austria. The world of the early abbeys is simply not
our world. Queen Matilda, who founded Caen, dedicated her
daughter to it at birth, and the daughter grew up to be abbess as the
day follows the night. Her sister as dowager Countess of Blois
became a nun at Marcigny; her name was Adela. I strongly suspect
that it was just such women who embroidered the Bayeux tapestry,
rather in lamentation than in triumph. It is terribly like a winding
sheet.

Marcigny was founded by St Hugh, one of the two powerful
Abbots of Cluny who ruled that community between them for the
entire eleventh century. He was a count's son, and kinsman to the
Duke of Aquitaine, a monk at sixteen, prior at twenty-four and
abbot at twenty-five. By the time of his death Cluny had two
thousand subject houses and associated houses, and the biggest
church and monastery in the world, consecrated by the Pope in
1095. Marcigny was therefore a small matter to him. He built it in
1055 for his mother and sister and their friends. They elected the
Blessed Virgin as perpetual Abbess, which disposed of one problem,
but Hugh insisted that it was governed in practice by him. The nuns
are said to have been more austere than the monks. Sometimes a
single old lady contrived to install herself in a men's abbey, and that
is no doubt the sort of thing that any abbot of the period would have
wished to avoid. One has the impression that in older, warmer days
an abbot would have welcomed it: as Eve Crispin installed herself
at Bec under Anselm, the second abbot, and became a general
mother to the community.

In the twelfth and thirteenth centuries and later, the women's
houses were like the smallest stars in the sky, very numerous but
hard to observe because they lack magnitude. They did not always

last long. Robert of Arbrissel, who was born about 1047, became a hermit and then a wandering preacher. Sad to say, he was one of the preachers of the first Crusade. But he spent most of his time setting up small groups of penitents, some of which developed into orders of monks and nuns. After 1096 he founded a community dedicated to the Virgin, with the religious widow of a local nobleman as her earthly representative. This was Fontevrault which grew to be a well-organized and aristocratic women's institution, in which women ruled over men. The sober grandeur of its architecture still conveys what it once was. Duke William of Aquitaine, the first troubadour, and his granddaughter Eleanor, the widow of King Henry II of England, lie buried there. This strange mixture of wild wandering hermits, enthusiastic penitents, and royal families is somehow a mixture of essential ingredients without which the growth of monasteries, male or female, and of the friars' orders that followed, cannot be well understood.

Norbert of Xanten, the founder of the Premonstratensian Order, the Canons of Premontre, is an important link between the settled monks and the friars. He found himself at the head of a mixed Order in the early twelfth century, which by the mid-century is supposed to have had ten thousand women members, though the canons soon put a stop to the recruiting of women. The growth of this Order is yet another curious mixture of wild, wandering preacher and institutional growth of a more organized kind. The charismatic side did not really last long, and in the end, as in so many examples, the men were relieved to get rid of the women. The women fought back. Las Huelgas near Burgos is a splendid abbey, socially a Spanish equivalent of Fontevrault only almost more beautiful. It was founded by Eleanor, Queen of Castile, the daughter of Henry II of England and his Eleanor, to house the royal tombs, and she and her husband lie buried there. The abbesses were great ladies, and although they claimed to be Cistercians they refused to obey the General Chapter of the Cistercians, because no woman was permitted to be a member of it. The details of Las Huelgas combine Romanesque and Islamic elements. It is a strange place to find the arms of England emblazoned on a tomb.

What were called the Beguines have some importance in this discussion, precisely because they were not very organized. They were religious ladies without any elaborated rules or permanent vows or much fuss at all. Being women, they had the advantage of not being so much regulated by Rome. They spread from Liège and Flanders to Cologne and the banks of the Rhine. By the fourteenth century they were all over Northern Europe, though they made little progress in England or France, where unregulated houses of women were not well viewed. The vast increase of women's orders down to the twentieth century under increasing regulations proves that whatever the social and spiritual or personal needs these Orders meet, they have nothing really to do with institutional life. Women did not cease to want to be religious simply because the institutional doors were closed to them, nor did they want to be unorganized or impermanent. That was simply how things happened. In Belgium as it now is, where the Cistercian Abbot of Villers was nicer to them than other Cistercians, Cistercian nuns flourished.

Bridget of Sweden was a visionary who married at fourteen and bore eight children, one of them St Catherine. Her visions began when she was already thirty-two and a lady in waiting to the queen, in 1335. She then made pilgrimages, and her husband died on one, at the Cistercian abbey of Alvastra. She stayed on there for three years, until she was forty-three. She then founded a monastery of her own on Lake Vattern for sixty nuns and twenty-five monks, with two enclosures but one church. The only luxury they were allowed was books. I think this was the first genuinely bookish religious order; individuals in the early medieval orders never had very many books, but Bridget's nuns and monks could each have as many as they liked. It was one of the premonitory rumblings of the Renaissance. All superfluous income was given to the poor. After three years, Bridget wandered off to Rome, but her monastery went on prospering and the King of Sweden liked it. Vadstena was its name. Bridget did a lot of prophesying and dire warning, and the published version of her vision is heavily edited and extremely grim. But she did try to stop the King mounting a crusade against the local pagans. Her religious order never had more than seventy houses, but it still has a convent in Devonshire that can boast of an unbroken continuity from the last nuns of Syon Abbey, founded by Henry V. The monks of the order died out.

A few more general points about women's religious orders may be worth making, though they are obvious enough. A lot of monks have entered monasteries because they were too bookish or retiring for normal life. Dunstan is an example, so is Hugh of Cluny, who was too physically awkward to be a knight. The same is true of nuns, if they could not or would not marry. Money comes into it with both sexes, the clergy being a famous solution for younger sons, but more so probably with women. In both cases there is a curious interweaving with heroic literature and its ideals adapted to religious life, with the literature of chivalry and romance and courtly love at a later period, and no doubt with the Romantic movement in relatively modern times. Women in abbeys were patrons of just the same arts as men, but I know nothing about women's manuscripts except in the case of Hildegard, and the suspicion that the nuns at Winchester would bear investigation. In the later Middle Ages nuns contributed little to Latin and may not have known it well, but Hroswitha, a German nun in the high medieval period, wrote a Latin comedy which no medieval man ever equalled. Still, it is true that if nuns were poets they were so on a minor scale in their vernacular languages. I have no idea why this should be, unless it was because they were denied the opportunity of performance.

As for modern nuns, they are wiser and warmer than monks, and much more vulnerable. They are more human altogether. The occasional exceptions to this are wearing a mask which ill becomes them.

The Charterhouse

Carthusians have always had extraordinary charm, though one can count on one's fingers the times one has ever come across one, because they are the most deeply drowned in silence and the most secluded of all monks. The old Jesuit under whom I was put for a year after ordination had once been a Carthusian, and he still had something of their quality. (The Jesuits have an ancient treaty with the Carthusians by which any Jesuit can go and join a Carthusian community at any time, without breaking his existing vows, and without anyone's permission.) I recollect his teaching us that the Carthusian way of meditating was not in the series of drill positions, standing and kneeling and sitting by turns, that we had all learnt as novices, nor the cloistral walking that I preferred, but lying full length resting on one elbow. This explains a recurring image of meditation in seventeenth-century painting.

The problem of being a Carthusian is double. One has to be perfectly obedient while living almost completely unobserved, and one has to have the digestion of a camel, because food comes once a day, and when it comes one must eat enough of it. Also one has to operate on very little sleep. There are few other problems. Carthusians live alone in little cottages round a cloister; they cultivate their own small gardens and meet only for the chanting of the office, except on very few days in the year. They vote with black and white beans. A doctor to a Carthusian priory told me that they have almost no diseases, and live to be very old. Some time after eighty, they just go out quietly like candles. An old Carthusian did go to a hospital I knew once, for hernia I believe. All the nurses fell in love with him. He got himself cured by a miracle from heaven and went back to his cell. The senior monk who came to fetch him gave him a wigging for not having his miracle at home.

If you are going to become a Carthusian, you probably do not care where, but personally I would care. At the Grande Chartreuse, the cloister is enclosed against the fiendish Alpine weather, the roofs are high-pitched, and the cloister grass is like a controlled lake, lapping the walls of the mortuary. You could imagine the spirit of Calvin at no great distance, though you would have the mountains and the forests to compensate. But the Certosa of Florence, which now has a useful but lamentable road very near it, not only used to be delightfully hard to get to, but had a marvellous, open Renaissance cloister, with some kind of garden and a few monuments. Just enough, that is the point. One is always nosing around for a way of life which is enough, but just enough.

Admittedly the Certosa of Florence when I saw it had very few monks and its sacristy was crusted with ornamental woodwork, from which a deadly infestation of specially virulent woodworms spread to the whole city. The monk I spoke to was very proud of those woodworms.

I dreamed for twenty years, not very intensely I admit, of ending up in the Certosa of Florence. The Carthusian vocation is to desire nothing but God. All true religion has that streak in it.

The London Charterhouse under Henry VIII behaved with their usual peaceful courage. They had a vision during a Mass of the Holy Spirit, and all agreed to be hanged, and were, without any fuss on their part. I like to imagine that Thackeray's Colonel Newcome owes just a touch or two to the Carthusians. The London Charterhouse today must be one of the most neglected and touching monuments in London. There is one Carthusian community in England still, lost in rural Sussex. Pope Pius XII made them go for walks in pairs and have conversation one afternoon a week. They said at the time that it was their greatest penance. And they were made to have communal cooking. They used to cook their rations alone, but the Prior complained that in practice that meant some of them ate raw food, and others spent all day inventing the perfect way to cook a potato.

The Carthusian order combines the hermit's ideal with the stable community. The letters of some of the earliest Carthusians, which are all of course exercises on holy themes, have survived. The best ones are "Invitations to the desert", as they used to be called, addressed to friends in the world. The one by St Bruno himself to Raoul le Verd is marvellous, but somehow too dazzling, too enveloping. My favourite is by Guigues, who was in some ways more practical and less messianic. He had no use for introductions or transitional phrases, he just argued along in a straight line. They are both of them like good old men in Shakespeare. They are not sententious, but they have a simplicity, a rustic solemnity. Guigues finishes his letter like this:

> . . . . *finem igitur et modum habeat epistola quem nunquam circa te caritatis habebit affectio.*

> . . . . so let my letter have a limit and an end, which my affectionate feeling for you will never have.

Guigues can write in a way that permits jokes, and is supple enough for personal expression. "Persuading towards peace and quiet is a cheerful subject." *Felix quidem materia est, suadere otium.* He speaks of "panting for what is heavenly" both in the letter and in his private thoughts, and he really seems to have done so. Bruno is more mystical maybe, but at that time the modern distinction between ascetic and mystical did not exist. It was assumed that the purpose of a monk's life was mystical.

Other early Carthusians are not always so charming, however their phrases may strike home. "O hope O love O enjoyment of time's kingdom, how empty . . ." says John of Portes. There is no difference of sincerity, but one does not believe him as one believes Guigues or Bruno. When the account of Bruno's death imitates the very words of the Gospel, one is not affronted. "Knowing that his hour had come to pass out of this world to the Father, he called together his brethren and gave an account of all the stages of his life since his childhood, and then in a long and deep discourse explained his belief in the Trinity, and so concluded . . ." The conclusion was the seventh-century Creed of Toledo. "On the next day which was the Lord's day that holy soul was freed from his body." I find myself believing every word of it.

Monastic Politics

There is no world without politics, and the constant politics of such big and powerful institutions as the monasteries became in the central Middle Ages was inevitable. Their own internal politics, monastery against monastery and communities divided against themselves, were at least equally virulent and more shocking. But when one enters into detail, the description is sufficiently revealing to remove the shock.

One must remember that monasteries are intended to foster our desire for change: they are full of missionary spirit. Change involves an exercise of power, and where there is power there are politics. Institutions by an instinct of self-defence tend to cannibalize or otherwise consume their internal missionaries, but sometimes one breaks loose. The new theology and philosophy and the beginnings of science, and even the recovery of the pagan classics were nourished by monasteries before they broke on the world, though one can no more distinguish the monks as typical members or as makers of their age in the eleventh and twelfth centuries than one can distinguish the foam from the solid water of the breaking wave. The pope who preached the First Crusade (1088) was a monk of Cluny. The previous pope (1086–7) was the abbot of Monte Cassino.

Monte Cassino, the old abbey of Benedict, depended heavily on the Normans in southern Italy; whenever the Normans had good relations with the popes, which was more often than used to be supposed, Monte Cassino was close to the papacy. The end result of this conflict was that monastic communities trained or founded by Monte Cassino and La Cava carried their reformations and austerities far to the south and into Sicily, where they drove out the Greeks. But the infamous or merely inevitable story goes back to Desiderius and earlier. In 1084 the Normans had "rescued" the Pope and burned Rome. It was Desiderius as abbot who put his monks under the protection and patronage of Robert Guiscard; he never wavered from that policy, and his order reaped its harvest. It was hard to see what else he could have done, if his first political duty was really to his own monks.

There is no doubt that Cluny was just as politically minded, so one is not surprised to hear that politics were its downfall in the lifetime of the next generation. The details of what happened, which the Cluny chronicles had virtually obliterated from history, were uncovered only in 1984. An abbot called Hugh took the wrong, that is the losing, side in the papal schism of 1159, one of those enlivening periods of popes and anti-popes. It is important to notice that every abbot of Cluny in the years following the death of Peter the Venerable (1157), who was a young, fire-eating reformer and grew old on his throne, was elected old, none of them reigned long, they were experienced men from subject monasteries, often old diplomats who knew the European courts, and sometimes noble or royal by birth. The Abbot Hugh was the only successful internal candidate in these elections.

One can observe a little of his quality as a prior, before his fatal elevation. A monk had died in a subject monastery, and three coins, not worth much, perhaps, were found in his clothes. They refused the poor old fellow Christian burial. Hugh the Prior then most fortunately had a vision. The dead monk appeared to him and showed him a letter signed Jesus, which said he was forgiven. His Christian burial, or presumably reburial, could therefore take place.

Hugh had backed the German Emperor's pope, and failed to change sides dexterously or swiftly enough. The Pope's emissaries went to Vézelay, a subject house, instead of Cluny. Pontius the

Abbot of Vézelay was Peter the Venerable's brother; he would, it appears, have succeeded Hugh had he not died in 1161, but the consequence of his policy was that in 1162 Vézelay was set free from Cluny by papal decree, and became independent. As for Hugh, he was deposed, becoming in retrospect an anti-abbot like an anti-pope, and fled to the Emperor, where he was said to have "usurped" a Cluniac priory. Yet, as the Archbishop of Mainz pointed out in a letter, if Hugh had not acted as he did, Cluny would have lost all those of her possessions and dependencies over which the Emperor had any power.

One has the impression that these vast monastic families, even though they were not strictly speaking unified organizations, and although their influence went far beyond their own subject houses, were continually fighting for their lives, and that the battle was a losing one. Also they do seem to have cared more for their institutional life than they did for the monk with the money, or for Hugh the anti-abbot. Hugh is recorded to have submitted at Venice in 1177, but I do not know where he died. It may well be that these events are best understood as just part of the history of the Normans and of Europe. It may be that one should think of the monks of Cluny only in terms of their spiritual influence and their extraordinary stone monuments: the carvings of Vézelay, for example. Their reforming influence on other houses independent of them certainly spread to Monte Cassino, to La Cava dei Tirreni near Salerno, and through them to Rome itself and to Sicily. Monastic orders are like hermit crabs, they occupy old shells. The reform of Cluny had its effect even in England. But Cluny was superseded by new reforms and other ways of life.

Monte Cassino differed from Cluny in many ways, though its influence and prestige were similar. Three of its monks became reforming popes, but its consolidated lands and the protection of the Normans made the monastery itself rather independent of papal demands. It founded no new religious order and followed no new fashions in liturgy. It was confident of its own antiquity, which is hardly surprising, and the writings of its monks were untainted by the somewhat odious moral fervour of the North. It cultivated the small local saints of southern Italy, gave house-room to the first medical translations from Arabic, and built the wonderful cathedral of Salerno. Between Cluny and Monte Cassino the similarities are at least as striking as the differences. They are separated by geography, nationality and intellectual climate. In both of them, the night office went on being sung, and the seasons of the liturgy merged into a liturgy of the seasons.

St Albans

The Abbey of St Albans was a wealthy royal foundation, and its magnificent buildings, like Jumièges and Caen in Normandy and Winchester and Durham (a little later) in England, were essentially the result of the amazing constructive energies of the Normans, which were almost greater than their destructive energies, one must admit. The style is similar in all examples, so where one place has not survived one may study the others. St Albans is where it is because of St Alban, and because of what survived of Roman Verulamium and its road system. It was founded about 793 and refounded about 970, so it was ancient as well as royal. Verulamium had been a town before the Romans came, and the martyr's shrine of St Alban was famous in Europe long before the Abbey was founded there. The Abbey was a centre of patronage in the arts for many centuries; the style of its manuscripts is often identifiable, and there is even a special sculptural style in baptismal fonts connected with St Albans.

Its annual income as reckoned by King Henry's commissioners in 1535 was above £2,102 a year, the highest of any Benedictine monastery in England except for Westminster Abbey and the

Cathedral Priory of Canterbury. Reading had £1,938 a year, Crowland had £1,093, and Gloucester £1,430. The Priory at Great Malvern had £380, and Barnstaple £123. A dozen Cistercian nuns and some lay brothers at Baysdale in Yorkshire had £20 a year, though the nineteen at Nun Appleton, about whom Marvell fantasized in his poem, had £73. There had once been thirty of them. A London hospital would have two or three hundred. St Bartholomew's had £305, and Bedlam had above £277 in 1632. The number of monks at St Albans is never recorded to have risen above 54, though the statutory limit was set at 100 monks in about 1200. The original foundation had nuns as well as monks. At the refoundation in 969 nuns were somehow reintroduced, perhaps unofficially. They seem to have been more than once confined to the Abbey almshouses, but they continued in existence until 1150, when Sopwell Priory was built to house them on their own. Sopwell had been an old hermitage lived in by two old holy ladies. In 1330 it had about 19 nuns, and in 1535 about 9, with an income of £40. The St Albans monks had not been over-generous.

In 1380 St Albans had 54 monks, 2 novices and 2 lay brothers. On their income, they will have had too many servants to need many lay brothers, but two is not many. Reading had 65 monks in 1305, but then the numbers sank. Westminster once had 80 or more, sinking to fewer than 50. St Albans always seems to have had some number between 46 and 54, which appears to be normal for a successful Benedictine abbey in the later Middle Ages when other orders were competing for novices. Just before the suppression, before any monks had started to melt away, St Albans had 46 monks in residence and 6 student monks at Oxford, where St Albans was wealthy and high-handed enough to maintain a house of its own.

One of the greatest contributions to English life that St Albans made was in the continuity of its chronicles. The importance of monastic chronicles at a time when history could not be properly written was considerable, and the monks in every generation had studied some of those classical historians on whom the science of history was in the end refounded. They were often sharp observers of personality, as is natural in an enclosed community, and, given the nature of medieval societies, they were often in a position to comment sensibly on great events. But they were chroniclers; they dealt with the events of their own times as they affected their own monasteries, and with the wider world only for its resonance in that small place. This gives them a further advantage of clear and conscious focus. But having said all that I must own that they did not write what we are used to calling history, and in reading them one certainly feels a lack. Still, it is something that when most monastic chronicles died out in the course of the thirteenth century, feeling themselves dwarfed perhaps by the scale of the world, St Albans produced Roger Wendover, Matthew Paris, and their followers, with one gap of about forty years after 1265. These years were made up in a later work by a monk who seems to have spent thirty years preparing to compose his treatise, so the gap is more apparent than real.

Matthew Paris is well thought of by medieval historians today, and David Knowles believed that Thomas of Walsingham, Precentor of St Albans around 1380, was fit to rank with him. He wrote a sequel to Matthew Paris, and a short account of English history from 911 to 1419, which has been called "the best history of England produced in the Middle Ages". Useful as these writers may be to modern historians, and fascinating as insights into the medieval mind, I cannot pretend to have been delighted by them, or to have any wish to reopen their works, except for the *Gesta Abbatum*, the Deeds of the Abbots down to 1255, by Matthew Paris. It is the rather full portraiture of Paris and Walsingham that lies behind some of the most fascinating pages of David Knowles: on the Abbot Thomas de la Mare, for example, whom one comes to know as if he were an academic colleague. One even comes to imagine one can sense characteristics in common with his collateral descendants in this century.

Thomas Walsingham was a classicist, like others of his day, and although the Renaissance had not yet visited England, if it ever did except as calligraphy, he tackled typical Renaissance subjects. He wrote a commentary on Ovid's *Metamorphoses*, with an account of the origins of the gods. However unclassical and counter-Renaissance his earnest views may be, the writing of that commentary must have been a pleasure to him, and an education of a strange kind. He seems to have shown interest in Dictys of Crete, a pretended eyewitness account of the Trojan war which is still readable though seldom read, and in the Alexander romance, a highly entertaining story, popular in nearly all countries, times and languages throughout the Middle Ages, now neglected. These interests of Thomas of Walsingham suggest a taste on the cheerful side for a monk, more donnish than monkish. But his Latin is awful, flowery and full of false rhetoric.

He appears to have been an example to John Whethamstede, and perhaps his teacher. John was born in 1393 and would have been twenty-two at the time of Agincourt, but by then he was already Prior of students at Gloucester College, Oxford, the monastic house now called Worcester, which has left its name only to Gloucester Green bus station. He then served as Prior of St Albans, and in 1420 he became Abbot at twenty-seven. This preposterously early appointment may be a measure of his intellectual brilliance and the value placed on such things by that elite community, and to the prestige of Thomas of Walsingham's writings, but one would have thought it would end in tears, and that is what happened. He was immediately plunged into great matters outside his Abbey. Before Henry V went to France he fulfilled his dead father's promise by founding Syon Abbey. In 1421 he came home, toured England, and set about the reform of Benedictine monasteries. The St Albans chronicles speak of "allegations of false brethren", partly justified because of recent deaths bringing "uncontrolled youth" into power. The Carthusian Prior of Mount Grace in Yorkshire is said to have influenced the King; he was Robert Layton, a former Benedictine monk. John Whethamstede was one of the six Benedictine delegates to meet the King's three commissioners, one of whom was Layton, after the King's speech in the Chapter House at Westminster, while Parliament held its session in the Painted Chamber. The King told the monks that his ancestors and others had valued the prayers of men of austere and disciplined lives. If the monks resumed their discipline, the prayers would become as effective as they once had been. I must regret that Shakespeare knew nothing about this scene. A committee was appointed.

John Whethamstede drafted and read out the counter-proposals of the monks. Nothing much happened, but he made some gentle reforms at St Albans and seems to have been trusted outside his home ground, since in 1423 he went with the English delegation to Pisa and Siena representing the Benedictines, and Archbishop Chichele commissioned him to write to the Pope in the name of all the English clergy. Such decisions are a fine balance between the weight of institutions and positions and the intellectual weight of the individual. In 1426 he was elected President of the Benedictines in England, and was regularly re-elected until 1438, when he was forty-five. He was financially capable and an energetic builder. He put a special official in charge of the Abbey fabric and set up an emergency fund with a definite, specified income. He was active in litigation on behalf of the Abbey, and very often successful at it. In fact he was like the head of a modern Oxbridge college who would be considered a success. He was also much like that in his literary work, which at the time must have appeared more distinguished than it does today.

In 1441 he resigned his abbacy, had himself pensioned off to his native village, where he rebuilt the manor house and bought land, and tried to bury himself in literature. This was an unusual, almost a unique step for an abbot to take. He gave his own reasons as being that all was well and he could retire gracefully, in view of the troubles he had been through, his complicated ill-health, and his embarrassing habit of blushing in public. Some historians have suspected secret political reasons, to do with the waning influence of Humfrey Duke of Gloucester, his special protector. David Knowles thought the trouble was his failure in an attempt to reform the house at Redburn, which the monks used for holidays, and where rules of diet, for example, could be ignored. He further

suspected that John Whethamstede was "a neurotic, with the combination of energy, obstinacy, and avoidance of reality that is so
often found in such a one". Personally I think the poor man just
had a crazy wish to be a famous scholar as well as all the other
things, and at forty-eight he was ready for a quiet life with simple
amenities, to which the world had accustomed him but the Abbot's
lodgings did not provide. And maybe he did feel ill.

What is even more extraordinary than his resignation is that he
was persuaded to stand for election again at the death of his own
successor. The successor had reigned ten years, he was a bully, and
in his shadow two brothers called Wallingford had become politically
important in the Abbey; there was suspicion of embezzlement, and
William Wallingford was a candidate for the abbacy. John
Whethamstede was elected and ruled St Albans for another fifteen
years until his death at seventy-two, old for those days, and loved
and lamented by all. He does not sound neurotic. In 1461 after one
of the battles of the Wars of the Roses the town was devastated and
so were the Abbey lands. For a time the monks scattered, and the
Abbot lay quiet in a country manor, but he saw to it that the privileges of the Abbey were confirmed by the new king. In his first term
of office, which was more active as one would expect, John
Whethamstede spent £2,334 on construction and furnishings in the
Abbey church and monastery buildings, though this includes a big
bill for repairs. He spent even more on the town and manorial
property of the monastery, and £1,362 on new property. The in-
ventory of treasures of St Albans for the mid-fifteenth century is
very rich indeed.

David Knowles is rather hard on John Whethamstede. "It is
impossible to regard him as a great man", he says. But is that a fair
remark? He was a successful and, it seems, popular man of affairs,
not his first vocation, within the limits of the not negligible world in
which he operated. We do not even know that he was lax as a monk.
As for the significant failure over the holiday house, I remember a
remark of Trollope's Warden that things were better on the whole
in the days when whist was played in the Bishop's Palace at

Barchester. I do not expect that what went on was very scandalous, and if one found it so one could always retire to Mount Grace and become a Carthusian. One cannot live other people's lives for them or save their souls, even if one is an abbot. And in the end one cannot hold back the tide of the times, though one may be wise and courageous to try. He did try. The first confrontation with Henry V is fascinating, but the King's detailed proposals are not recorded. It was a mistake to form a committee. One cannot help wondering whether if Henry V had been successful, Henry VIII might have had to leave the Benedictines alone. He did not even leave the Carthusians alone, all the same.

Professor Knowles is on stronger ground when he says that "The writer of Whethamstede's letters and verses cannot have been a man of true simplicity, or even a man of powerful and direct intelligence." He visited Italy at the height of the Renaissance without noticing what was going on. His verses in Latin are unmetrical and at times ungrammatical. Perhaps one should think of him as of a bright and well-intentioned schoolboy in a very bad school, who never had the opportunity to learn. That is how the first English "humanists", as they are wrongly called, grew up. Monastic education ruined their relation with the vernacular language, England had no Dante, and Chaucer was not commonly read in monasteries, or we would have more manuscripts. The Latin learnt in monasteries was more laboriously learnt with every generation, and its ideals were disastrous in both prose and verse. Even the handwriting of his boyhood was extremely ugly.

John Whethamstede was criticized for working too hard at literature. It is probable that some of his many writings are still unknown, or unidentified. We have part of his *Granarium*, of which the Duke of Gloucester gave a complete copy to Oxford in 1444. It was a sort of encyclopedia of morals, events, and personalities, down to recent ones, including the trial of Wyclif. He used classical sources wherever they existed and were available to him. In contrast with this "grain-barn" of earnest information, he wrote a "chaff-bin of the poets", which was 700 articles on classical mythology, almost all cribbed from Boccaccio's *Genealogies of the Gods*, which is not to be confused with his more entertaining works. His "food cupboard of the poets" is just a collection of tags from poetry, some of it medieval but most of it classical. It is of no possible use to anybody. The most interesting bits of all this back-breaking production are articles about contemporary theories of church government in his encyclopedia. He knew a lot about that.

He was not a devout, enthusiastic monk of the early generations of his, or of any order. How could he have been? His monks were not like an early Irish community of hermits. How could they have been?

> A little pool but very clear
> To stand beside the place,
> Where all men's sins are washed away
> By sanctifying grace.
>
> My choice of men to live with me
> And pray to God as well;
> Quiet men of humble mind –
> Their number I shall tell.
>
> Two by two my dozen friends –
> To tell the number right –
> Praying with me to move the King
> Who gives the Sun its light.
>
> A lovely church, fit home for God,
> Bedecked with linen fine,
> Where over the white Gospel page
> The Gospel candles shine.
>
> And all I ask of housekeeping
> I get and pay no fees;
> Leeks from the garden, poultry, game,
> Salmon and trout and bees.

This is from Frank O'Connor's version of a fourteenth-century Irish poem. It would have been an ideal as distant from John Whethamstede as it is from us. No doubt Frank O'Connor has added certain touches of nostalgia, and perhaps the original was no more than a nostalgic exercise. But it rings true in a way. The monks of the Middle Ages were not able to choose the world they lived in, any more than we are, and however such a poem may ring true, it did not offer a real alternative to John Whethamstede, or perhaps to anybody. And yet the number twelve is suggestive. It is twelve like the twelve apostles, and in the Cistercian Order it was always twelve monks who went out to found a new house, and the cloister often had twelve doors. Even the theme of natural beauty, which in some stanzas of the poem is too florid to quote, occurs with similarly unnatural rhetoric in Walter Daniel's *Life of Aelred*, where the leaves at Rievaulx whisper in symphony and the birds sing in descant. The poem may be of Cistercian origin, and it may really express how people thought they felt. At any rate, it is a far cry from St Albans.

Serbia

The monasteries of Serbia cast a fascinating shadow on the epic folk songs that have survived there from the period just after the fall of Serbia to the Turks in the fifteenth century. Some of these heroic poems reflect an earlier world; it is almost unique in Europe for so powerful and genuine an illiterate poetry to survive. In these poems forests are haunted places, terrible messages are delivered by birds, and a letter is called a little book, the village singers through whom the poems were transmitted never having seen a letter.

Serbia was Christianized by missionaries sent out from Rome at the request of the Byzantine emperor, but the process was superficial, and they had to be re-Christianized in the ninth century. Both the Serbs and the Bulgarians accepted Christianity at that time as part and parcel of accepting Byzantine protection. Their monastic traditions are therefore Orthodox. Anyone who has heard the unaccompanied singing of Bulgarian monks must have felt the life of those inaccessible Balkan monasteries to be among the most impressive surviving monuments of Orthodoxy. The language of the liturgy was a version of the Macedonian Slav dialect, expanded under pressure of translation from the Greek. The language of the folk songs is Serbo-Croat. The liturgical language was the first written language of the Slavs; its two alphabets were invented for the purpose of converting them, which was entrusted to two brothers from Saloniki, one a great linguist and administrator, the other a monk, Constantine (later called Cyril) and Methodios.

The natural monastic centre of the Balkans was Athos, the Holy Mountain, and one hears of sainted monarchs retiring there, though they tend to re-emerge. But these holy kings, like the Anglo-Saxon and Norman kings of England, liked to found monasteries of their own, and for similar reasons. They were dynastic monuments, and the royal parliaments (Sabori) would be summoned to celebrate their foundation. The folk songs clearly reflect the motivation of the kings, at least as the people understood it. In the course of its development, the Serbian kingdom approached more and more closely to a Greek model, particularly in its religious institutions.

We have two versions in poetry of the building of Ravanitsa, a monastery founded in historical fact by Prince Lazar, but the poems imitate a Greek legend about the building of Hayia Sophia, in which the first intention of building it with gold and silver and gems was abandoned because the Last Times were coming. The Prince's wife upbraids him:

> The old Nemanjichi who once were,
> reigned on the earth and passed on,
> they gathered up no riches in heaps,
> they built the buildings of the soul,
> they made many monasteries,
> they built up High Dechani,
> Dechani which is near Djakovitsa,
> the Patriarchate above flat Pech,
> and white Devich in Drenitsa,

and the church of Peter by Pazar,
over above the Pillars of St George,
Sopochani above cold Rashka,
the Trinity in Herzegovina,
and Janaja's Church in Vlach, in old Vlach,
and Pavilitsa below Jadovnik,
Studenitsa below Bervenik,
Zhitcha church above Karanovats,
the church of St Petka in Prizren,
Grachanitsa on level Kosovo,
all of these are the buildings that they built.

It is interesting that such a formidable list should exist in
traditional poetry, as its existence implies what can be shown by
other arguments, that these monasteries and churches were a symbol
of national identity, particularly under the Turks. The Princess
fears that her riches will not be "for our health or our souls' health,
neither for us nor any of our blood" unless they are spent on a
monastery. The poem goes on to prophesy the coming of the Turks.
"Our building of the soul shall serve for ever until the judgment of
God: not a stone shall be taken from a stone."

The other version of the poem gives a list of royal foundations
that includes monasteries, white churches, stone bridges, and
stone-paved roads. When the monastery was built,

the church flashed light like the bright sun,
it dazzled in the eyes of his white horse,
and the white horse reared up under the Tsar,
the white horse threw the Tsar from his saddle.
That place is called the Tsar's bump to this day,
so it was, and so it is to this day.

Most of the second poem is about builders and master craftsmen;
neither of them mentions monks even once. It was the buildings
themselves that were symbols. They were remote places built by
kings who were buried in them, but even the royal tombs left no
impression in popular poetry, though the frescoes sometimes did,
including the frescoes of kings. They are striking to this day; the
"massive blocks of honey-coloured stone" and "beautiful cliff of

greyish marble" at Studenitsa are still to be seen. The place is about
ten hours on foot from the nearest town.

Real monks do occur in popular poetry. In one splendid poem
Prince Marko's wife has been stolen. He disguises himself as a monk
and dances "a little monkish dance" in the course of which he cuts
off heads. In another, when Marko dies alone in a forest, an abbot
happens to pass by, as he might do in a Robin Hood ballad, which
some of these Serbo-Croat poems rather resemble. He is "Vasos of
Athos the Abbot, from Chilendarion the white-washed church",
with his attendant monk.

> He ties dead Marko on his own horse
> and carries him to the shore of the sea,
> he takes a boat with Marko dead,
> to carry him to the Holy Mountain.
> He brought him in to Chilendarion
> and he chanted for Marko dead
> the ceremony of mortality,
> he sang above his body on the earth
> in the white church of Chilendarion;
> and the old man buried Marko,
> he did not mark the stone over his grave,
> Marko buried shall never be known,
> there shall be no revenge taken on him.

Marko in fact is a hero who disappears like King Arthur, and
perhaps at one time Robin Hood, because his grave is not known.
He disappears as it were in a cloud of monastic incense, in the
ultimate refuge from the world, glimpsed from a great distance.
The Byzantine Greeks were much more closely conscious of their
monasteries, and their popular poetry reflects that consciousness.
"God, earth and heavens cry alarm, and Hayia Sophia, the great
monastery cries alarm; four hundred alarms, sixty two bells, for
every bell a priest, for every priest a deacon, here the King chants
and there the Patriarch, and at the vast chanting the pillars shook..."
This is a poem of only eighteen lines about the last Mass in
Constantinople, and the fall of the city to the Turks. "Do not weep
Lady for it will be yours, again with times and with the turn of
times."

When Constantinople was built, we hear in another Greek poem, "the angels took the water of the Holy Mountain, the earth of Chios, and the tiles of Adrianoupolis, and thus the angels built it and attend on it and protect it". It was monastic earth and water and tiles, I take it, that they used. The Byzantine quasi-identity of church and state extends into folk songs. Long after the fall of the city, the three monks of Athos and three monks of Crete who put out to sea with a Turk and a Jew and a little Greek sailor-boy – "with Christ is risen she was rigged, and launched with Lord have mercy" – still carry with them the sense of national identity.

San Lazzaro

The foundations of monasteries in comparatively modern times are curiously like and unlike the foundations of the past. They are in fact very much determined by the society of the time, and by climate and geography. Teresa of Avila was a successful foundress, as interesting a reformer as Bernard, and a magnificent mother superior. But Renaissance Spain was still in some ways feudal, which simplified her labours without lessening her troubles. She needed and possessed a very strong will indeed. John of the Cross was one of her easier conquests. He was introduced to her as a brilliant young prior just after his first Mass, and she enlisted him at once. I have never been quite certain that he ever knew what had hit him. He was after all a poet, a mystic, and the most genuine man in the world. One often feels that saints deserve a gentler fate.

One would expect the adventures of Mekhithar, the enlightened Armenian Abbot of San Lazzaro at Venice, which he founded in 1717, to be more sophisticated and less drastic. The island was an abandoned leper colony, and by granting it to Mekhithar the Senate avoided breaking the law against new religious communities in the city of Venice. Mekhithar was born at Sebaste and became a monk at fifteen. He travelled all over western Asia, settled at the monastery of Passen, met a Jesuit at Aleppo and set out for Rome, fell ill at Cyprus, and was ordained Doctor at the Convent of the Holy Cross, Sourp Nishan, near his native place. He visited Istanbul, ministered to the plague-stricken, and preached reunion with Rome. One must remember what a strong cobweb of relationships the Armenians had at that time all over Europe. The Armenian Church at Isfahan has a little museum of portraits of dignitaries, including one by Rembrandt of an Armenian priest in Amsterdam.

Mekhithar moved in 1703 to southern Greece, that is into the Venetian empire as it then was, with a straggle of disciples, and installed them at Modon on the southern spur of the west coast of the Peloponnese. There he built a monastery which no longer survives, and wrote a rule which he apparently wanted approved by the Pope. The Pope did approve the order, and Mekhithar as abbot, but insisted on the Rule of Benedict. Mekhithar had thought of the so-called "Rule of Augustine", another venerable Latin system. But in 1715 Modon was abandoned to the Turks, and the monastery was burnt and looted. The monks were lucky to reach Venice in April and to be settled in the ruins of San Lazzaro. They had always been interested in printing and translating, and their press became famous, almost more so than their monastery. They were essentially a community of exiles with their eyes and minds on the East. The monasteries of what is now Soviet Armenia, which I know only from photographs, are extraordinarily beautiful. The Venetian monastery is a typical Venetian building of the mid eighteenth century; it seems a world away. Soon after Mekhithar's death the community split, in a quarrel over discipline, and some of them went off to Trieste and then to Vienna, still doing similar work for dispersed Armenians.

Monastic and other religious orders have become more and more concerned with education since the Renaissance, and particularly since the European Enlightenment of the eighteenth century. Their educational activities have given them purpose and meaning, supported them financially, made them acceptable to the world, and fed them with potential novices. What are called teaching orders are now numerous. But the Armenians of San Lazzaro had their existence saved by their intellectuality. When Napoleon abolished monastic institutions in Venice, the Abbot of San Lazzaro, a Transylvanian Armenian nobleman with the Roman title of archbishop, was permitted to transform his monastery into an academy. When the Jesuit order was abolished by the Pope for a time, the English Jesuits simply called themselves the Gentlemen of Stonyhurst, and went on running their school. The Armenians in Venice reached their literary heights under a second archbishop abbot who took office in 1824, Sukias de Somal. The third, who was George Hurmuz, used to wear the insignia of Commander of the Iron Crown (Austria), Chevalier of the Légion d'honneur, and Italian, Turkish and Persian orders of similar grandeur. He must have lent a pleasing touch of farce to monastic life.

I have never been ashore at San Lazzaro, though to me it was a place of Byronic pilgrimage, and the only full description I have obtained was printed in the eighteen-seventies. It begins, "As soon as the iron prow of the Gondola touches the marble stairs which are laved by the clear waters of the Lagoon, the door of the Monastery opens as if by enchantment, and the visitor passes into the Atrium which is adorned with flowers and shrubs . . ." It sounds like Cipriani's. In the seventies there were sixty monks called doctors and some lay brothers. The monastic revenue came from printing, and the doctors had spread to Paris, Istanbul, and elsewhere.

The church was Gothic, and one of its monuments commemorated an old keeper of the leper house; another was put up to a school founded by his son, an East Indian Armenian, in the nineteenth century. "On great fete days one may witness all the pomp and splendour of the Armenian service." The library had 30,000 books. There was a small museum of Armenian antiquities. In fact the entire operation was like that of a thousand or more monastic and religious houses all over Europe in the eighteen-seventies, the last survivors of which I have known in many countries. The difference is that the Armenians were refugees as the Poles and the Czechs are in Paris and in London. But I know of no Polish or Czech monastery abroad founded since 1945, the reasons for that lack being probably economic. The San Lazzaro community had a certain nobility of style: their bust of the founder was by a pupil of Canova, they proudly exhibited ancient coins and a telescope and a bit of papyrus given by an Indian Armenian. Their manuscripts were catalogued in quarto, and they won prizes for printing at world exhibitions in Paris, London and so on. They published a learned journal, laboured at a dictionary, and ran a school and a seminary. Pope Pius VII visited them and Napoleon III sent his portrait. They used to fly an Ottoman banner presented by the Sultan on certain feast days. "One rarely encounters many Fathers in the Monastery, the majority are absent on missions to Constantinople, Asia, or France." Among the works they translated into Armenian were *Paradise Lost*, Young's *Night Thoughts*, and Buffon's *Natural History of Birds*. St Dunstan would have understood these monks perfectly well, but Bernard of Clairvaux would not have liked them.

Monks Through Foreign Eyes

One could reasonably claim today that monks attract little curiosity and less hostility, because religious passions have cooled. Since the British were more or less unique in Europe for two or three hundred years in having no monasteries, the view that our foreign travellers took of monks is of some interest, because only the British came as it were fresh, though of course not unprejudiced, to what they observed. The first British observers of Greek monks thought them exotic, but foreign tales were tales of wonders so they brought more credulity to Greek superstition than some of their ancestors had done to their own. But these were seamen. Those who merely crossed the Channel, Catholics aside, always seem to have been horrified by mendicant monks, persistent and not over-clean, at Boulogne. The abbey gate at Boulogne was painted as huge, baroque, yellow and crumbling, the essence of romantic tourism. Until late in the day, the English visited Rome with a sneer on their lips. One can feel it in a note to the Geneva Bible about Roman carriages, in a satire by Marvell, and in eighteenth-century letters. The change came in the course of the eighteenth century, and the French exiles from the Revolution had something to do with it. Yet in the child-hood of my mother, just before the 1914 war, French nuns in Harrow on the Hill took schoolgirls with them whenever they went out, for fear of being stoned in the street, so they said.

When Goethe went to Italy in the seventeen-eighties he scarcely noticed monasteries though he passed below them, squat among their fields or towering on their rocks. He was so drowned in aesthetic values that he doubtless despised them, and he sneered at the "tinsel decorations" of Italian worship. English aesthetes of the same period thought monks freakish and monasteries romantic, but English aesthetics were more advanced. Goethe was like a retarded schoolboy rushing to his first picture gallery at eighteen. He had no time for Italian monks, as a German, as a Protestant, or as an enlightened intellectual. His furthest concession to romance is to walk through Rome under a full moon. "The Colosseum looks especially beautiful. It is closed at night. A hermit lives in a small chapel and some beggars have made themselves at home in the crumbling vaults."

When he got further south, to Messina in Sicily, monks were unavoidable, because they were everywhere in the high society he liked to frequent, and a monk was deputed to show him around. He records two monks at a grand dinner, secretly mocked and openly humiliated by their enlightened hostess, and replying with impenetrable politeness. "Is your spoon too small? Let me send for

a bigger one! You gentlemen must be used to large mouthfuls!"
Goethe thinks these jokes, of which he records many, are very
funny, but he loses heart because, as he says, they look less funny
on the page. That they are in bad taste does not occur to him. On
another day,

> We went with the Abbé [his monk guide] to the Bene-
> dictine monastery. We entered a cell and he introduced us
> to a middle-aged monk whose melancholy and reserved
> features did not promise a very reserved conversation. He
> was, however, a gifted musician, the only monk who could
> master the enormous organ in the chapel. He began to play
> the admirable instrument, filling the remotest corners with
> sounds that ranged from the gentlest whisper to the most
> powerful trumpet blasts. If one had not already seen this
> man, one would have thought that such power could only
> be exercised by a giant; now, knowing his personality, we
> could only wonder that he had not, long ago, succumbed in
> such a struggle.

Goethe is insufferably patronizing about monks, and lamentably
incurious about just the details of monkish life that we would like
to know.

The disdainful view Gibbon took of the bare-foot friars chanting
on the Capitol is well enough known. It was extremely odd of him,
since the Romans after all had bare feet and chanted, and he would
not have liked the bloody splashing and grunting and heaving of
their sacrifices. The church of the Ara Coeli, to which he objected,
is to my mind one of the most beautiful places in the world, but
perhaps he did not really climb the steps to find out. He had learnt
from Montesquieu and other French writers an irony and a style,
and sought in history an area where they might be indulged. One
might also point out that the Vestal Virgins of the Romans were very
like an aristocratic convent of nuns. They were enclosed, they had
religious duties, their virginity was sacrosanct, and the ruins of
their house in the Forum have the look of convent ruins. Horace
used them as a metaphor for eternity. "My praise shall freshen
while the Capitol still knows the silent virgin and the Priest."

The monastic revival in England in the nineteenth century had romantic French roots. It smelt of lilies like a funeral parlour. But there was another, continuous strand of a sober colour, that of the exiled communities that had lived out their lives here and there on the French coast ever since the Reformation, waiting to come home. They did come home, and settled in remote places. The daughter-houses of French foundations have followed them since, and the growth of a Catholic middle class has encouraged their prosperity, though for their foundations they depended more than one might imagine on old-fashioned aristocratic patronage, and the classic motive of prayers for the soul of the founder and his family. I have not been able to find any balanced assessment of these revived monasteries in their early days; they appear to have inspired pure affection of a rugged kind. The lily-smelling type of revivalist was of course mocked by everybody, recently with some brilliance in A. N. Wilson's novel, *Gentlemen in England*. Even their biographies read like unconscious mockery, particularly when read aloud in modern monasteries. It is an awful thought that the poet Hopkins was ripe for such a revivalist abbey had they caught him early enough. The Jesuits made him suffer, but Father Ignatius of Llanthony would have destroyed him.

The English abroad were fairer to non-Christian monks, because they saw them with less prejudice. Beckford's account of monasteries in Spain is brilliant as literature, and well deserves to be reprinted. In his day, of course, monks had an exotic attraction, and landscape gardens alluded to them, people played at hermits, the real ruins of abbeys saw landscapes like pictures by Salvator Rosa grow up around them. It is hard now to dissociate Rievaulx and Fountains from a certain sense of the eighteenth century. But Beckford failed to get inside the skin of his monks, because he thought he knew already what was inside them. This goes for innumerable British accounts of foreign monasteries. They are strong on atmosphere and often brilliant in details, they have the power of first impressions. But they lack intimate familiarity. They are better out of Europe, where they sometimes understand that the monks know one thing and one thing only, and as observers they catch a gleam of that one thing. They are like literary critics of John of the Cross, awed by what his secret must be.

The cult of St Francis in Victorian England, which brought us numerous reprints of the charming anecdotes called *The Little Flowers of Saint Francis*, almost certainly derives from the romantic cult of Italy. It is to be found in Trollope and might well be found in Jane Austen. Ladies lie on couches reading Italian and seducing the affections of curates. I do not think they paid much attention to the astonishing realities and paradoxes of his life. They saw them as they saw their "Italian primitives", in gilt frames, or they remembered him by Giotto, flaking on a wall while the lizards baked in the sun outside. The barriers of the word "primitive" have been pushed back a long way since those days, nearly out of existence let us hope. But they saw him as innocent. All the same, they pretended that the last lines of his famous "Canticle of the Sun", which really is "primitive" and "innocent", did not exist. He was not associated with sin and redemption, but with love and nature and praise; he was a magic child. The Canticle begins like that, with the sun and the moon and water, but it ends with severe views about mortal sin and the punishment of sin in hell. Did their eyes glide over that, or what did they think?

Marco Polo has interesting observations to make about the holy men surrounding the Grand Khan. I believe he saw them as friars of a kind, "religious mendicants". First we have the Khan's palace at Shandu, then his herd of milk-white mares, then the ceremonies of the astrologers in bad weather, and lastly the mendicants, who are presumably the Buddhist monks. Nineteenth-century travellers confirmed what might appear to be Marco Polo's exaggerated numbers. Turner discovered 2,500 monks in one monastery.

> In this country there are great monasteries or abbeys, so extensive indeed that they might pass for small cities, some of them containing as many as two thousand monks. They wear better dress than the other people of the place, they shave their heads and beards, and they celebrate the festivals

of their idols with the utmost possible solemnity, with bands
of vocal music and burning tapers. Some of them are permitted to take wives.

He goes on to speak of a second religious order called *sensim*,
interpreted as priests of Fo by the commentaries. They seem to have
belonged to an Indian religion which Buddhists would regard as
merely schismatic. Since lamas universally wore yellow or red,
these *sensim* were not lamas.

> They observe severe abstinence and live most austerely,
> with no food but a kind of stalk, which they steep in warm
> water until the farinaceous part separates from the bran, and
> they eat it like that. They worship fire and the others think
> of them as schismatic because they do not worship idols. . . .
> They never marry at all. They shave their heads and beards
> like the others, and wear hemp clothing, black or dull-
> coloured. Even if it were silk, the colour would still be the
> same. They sleep on coarse mats, and live harder than any
> people in the world. But now let us talk about the great and
> wonderful acts of the supreme lord and emperor, Kubla
> Khan.

His descriptions are utterly external, they are not even theological.
He might be describing a tribe of speechless or stone-age people,
and he does not even know what language they speak. The fact of
their existence is curious enough to be recorded, and that is all. One
can easily imagine a description of Western monks through Eastern
eyes in similar terms; in fact I would be surprised if one does not
exist. And yet the mere fact that these communities of holy men
were there to observe, if one went far enough, really is the most
impressive thing about them. Maybe the same could be said of
Western monasteries. They are only witnesses to something inside
human beings that we do not understand. Why do they take such
care to differ from one another? They raise by their way of life
serious questions about the unity of human nature and the
knowledge of God.

One might expect less sympathy for foreign monks from Flaubert,
but his human sympathies run deeper than Marco Polo's. He is a

creature of nerves and senses and deep, instantaneous impressions, or so I imagine him. His visit to Egypt was not a long one, but his departure was dramatic, what with the tears at home, the agony of parting from his mother, the further tears all the way to Paris, and the whores when he got there. French monks would not have surprised or attracted him, except maybe the Trappists. But in Egypt his eyes were fresh. Here he is writing to his mother:

> Just the evening before, we had been in a monastery of dervishes where we saw one fall into convulsions from shouting Allah! These are very fine sights, which would have brought many a good laugh from M. de Voltaire. Imagine his remarks about the poor human mind! About fanaticism! Superstition! None of it made me laugh in the slightest, and it is all too *absorbing* to be appalling. The most terrible thing is their music.

He thought monasteries were the most serious thing in Egypt, though he took a poor view of the Coptic monks of Gebel el Teir, who

> have the habit, as soon as they see a boatload of tourists, of running down, throwing themselves into the water, and swimming out to ask for alms. Everyone who passes is assailed by them. You see these fellows totally naked rushing down their perpendicular cliffs and swimming towards you as fast as they can, shouting Baksheesh, baksheesh, cawadja christiani! And since there are many caves in this particular spot, echo repeats Cawadja, cawadja! Vultures and eagles were flying overhead, the boat was darting through the water, its two great sails very full.

Flaubert was delighted with the humiliation of these monks by the Islamic boatmen, with beating, mockery, curses and sexual innuendo. A lingering doubt remains whether the swimmers really were monks, or just village boys.

My own impression of monks abroad has only been of the extreme politeness and reserve of Buddhists, the curious mixture of charm of nature and readiness to growl, but on the whole the philosophic friendliness of old religious men from one end of Islam to the other, and the mighty, ridiculous stateliness of Greek abbots and abbesses. I recall their reception rooms with the threadbare, beautiful carpet and the unlikely ornaments, and the spoonful of jam like *loukoum*, the glass of water and the tiny glass of liqueur like hair-oil. Their manners are fine but lordly, the ladies more so than the men. Outside there is usually some sweet, faded old monk or nun prowling about among one and a half rose bushes, or sweeping inconsequentially, and their conversation is on a lower key and much more memorable. I regret knowing so little about Japanese monks, except so far as it is possible to know them through prolonged meditation of pottery and poetry.

Part 4

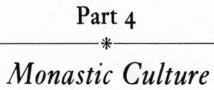

Monastic Culture

Stones

The monastic arts are mostly secular. To the builders and masons the monks supplied book-learning, and mystical theories of geometry and light. The art of calligraphy is secular and international; it flourished in monasteries and under their patronage because it was useful to the church and the state, although the self-expression of the monks, like the poetry and singing of the outside world, may well have been more powerful before the increase of literacy and the regulation of monastic music. The most precious treasures of monasteries, the elaborate reliquaries and the books studded with rock-crystal, were made by professionals and commissioned by the rich.

And yet the monks stamped a style on many of the arts, particularly on the stone sculpture of tombs and churches, where the graves of abbots differ greatly from those of crusaders. The crusaders with their crossed legs and swirling lines seem frozen from furious action, but the death of the abbots seems to express the truth of their lives. They have a sober propriety as if they were at home with death. The same may almost be said for the tombs of dead women, but that is perhaps because women in their lives were supposed to be as passive and limited as monks. The amazing height of Western monastic architecture is an international style that doubtless expresses the soul. It was not confined to monasteries. It arose, I think, from the re-use of classical monolithic columns, first it seems in Sicily and in Fatimid Egypt, and of course at Rome. But the new tall proportions were remoulded into a single coherent language as Gothic architecture, with stone that was easier to cut than the ancient marbles. Monastic architecture has a fluid lamenting grace. Even in ruins its last notes hang in the air.

Abbey architecture expresses mystery and majesty, and was meant to do so. Westminster Abbey was a place of pilgrimage and coronation, where the Norman kings were crowned and later monarchs lay in a horseshoe round the tomb of Edward the Confessor, climax and highest point of the long building. One would have to remove modern encumbrances to get a sense of that. The same system of the long church leading upwards to the pilgrim shrine is easier to feel at Le Puy in France, where the church crowns a steep hill. It is on the Compostela pilgrim route, of which one can buy maps in the local bookshops. At Winchester, English kings earlier than the Normans lie in the same horseshoe, but the shrine behind the high altar has been dismantled, and some of the tombs have only recently been rediscovered by excavation.

But as the Gothic style developed it became infinitely repeatable. The same fretted window forms of the fifteenth and sixteenth centuries that give such solemnity and richness to village churches were used indifferently in secular buildings, where they were carved in wood. They can be seen at Burford, or in the Lyme Regis museum, and they once lighted the wooden Whitehall of the Elizabethans. Since this late Gothic window seems to be a characteristic wood-carving style adapted with difficulty by masons, its origins may well be wooden and secular. In the same way the Norman crypt under Oxford castle mound shows that pillared, vaulted roofs are unlikely to have a monastic origin. They were functional, and belonged to the building technique of castles with which the Normans were so obsessed, needing as they did to feel safe from their oppressed tenants and from one another.

And yet. And yet. The physical presence of those abbeys that have survived in use, and of the ruins of others where the public may penetrate as freely as ghosts, walking through walls and wandering between centuries, gives so strong an impression that it can scarcely be ignored. Ruins can be mouldering, melancholy places. Wordsworth's "pastoral cottage, grass to the very door" may be one's favourite human dwelling, but a palatial monastic ruin where the grass is everywhere underfoot is another matter. How is it that these ruins seem to speak so simply and so eloquently? And the more that survives the more thrilling they are, particularly if a cloister and an altar survive. There is one small statue high up in the abbey ruins at Fountains that brings the whole place to life. A gravestone does the same at Rievaulx. The rock-hollowed monastic caves of Cappadocia are visibly crumbling away, and yet no human monument is stranger or more chilling; in a way, more moving. The blazing white Coptic monasteries at Wadi Natrun in Lower Egypt look like allegories of monastic frugality and mysticism. There is a convent outside Cairo, hard to visit now, being on the edge of a military area, as impressive on its modest scale as the greatest monastic monuments. In Cappadocia, the monks have eaten away the rock like termites, like wild bees or wasps, and in Western Europe they were still rearing up their massive stone monuments in the eighteenth century, as one can see at St Wandrille de Fontanelle; both kinds of elaboration are only the consequence of time, of aged institutions and the suppressed energy of monks. The essence of monastic art is simpler; it is an almost unconscious expression.

Old abbeys have long histories. Conques goes back to the eighth century. It accepted the Rule of Benedict in 795, and the building that survives is almost all in the pure, severe style of the eleventh century; it was finished a few years before 1066. Two of its towers were pulled down at the French Revolution and the stones looted, as at St Andrew's in Fifeshire, by the worthy citizens. In 1830 the church was restored by an architect who destroyed what remained of the cloisters. But Mérimée discovered Conques soon afterwards and saved what he could. For some inscrutable reason, the contents of the treasury, which are thrilling, seem to have remained intact throughout these adventures. Yet what excites me most about Conques is not its grandeur, its simplicity, beauty and height, nor even its troubled antiquity; it is one amazing, impassive stone angel in form like a Byzantine ivory, high up under the vaulting of the tower. This is a biblical, visionary figure, but its original meaning is not the point. The point is its solemnity, its sightless eyes, its handsome, economic ornament. It is like the statue of the Virgin which "expressionless, expresses God", but because the angel of Conques is part of a geometry and an architecture, and a life, it gives one a sharp sense of what monasteries were all about.

I must own here, I suppose, to being more impressed by older monasteries than those of the English Middle Ages, not because of their particular age but for their simplicity. One may feel the same about certain parish churches, of whatever period. The church of Kilpeck, for example, draws me again and again, not for its strangeness and freshness alone, nor for the problems it sets in art history, but because of the naivety mingled into the skill, and a rustic setting that somehow emphasizes its simple side. The setting of monasteries naturally plays on one's mind in the same way. Ile Barbe in the Rhône has been burnt, pillaged, dismembered and subdivided into private properties. There are bits of sculpture built into houses, and the crypt of the shrine of St Epipodus is in somebody's garden. But here a tower, there a bit of cloister, hint at what it once was. Charlemagne wanted to die there. Rocamadour on its crag is better known and in better condition. It is supposed to have been founded by Zachaeus, who climbed a sycamore tree to see Jesus, and had a head for heights. But I do not really like monasteries on crags, least of all Mont-Saint-Michel. There is a lurking complacency about them. The site of Lindisfarne with its freezing seal-haunted breakers seems more of a place to walk with God. This is a matter of austerity, of how little one needs.

The Greek Meteora are another matter. When I went there the road was new and intrusive, and I chose to climb up by a path, much as the founding father must have done. The day was hot and dusty and my watch stopped so that I lost all sense of time, a useful beginning for any monastic visit. I arrived extremely hot and exhausted, and the shade and cold water were to me the perfect refreshment. The Meteora are very high, certainly, but living up there is not so much like dwelling on a cliff-top as on a cloud. They are the shape of enormous petrified clouds. Meteora means midair, and the monks and all their things used to be drawn up in nets, which I have seen in use. I have never in my life so strongly experienced the sense of being in another world as in the Meteora. There were few monks then, and I think nearly as few nuns somewhere nearby, but you could feel the monastic spirit as you could breathe the air. I think this was a matter of very simple elements: the wooden rattle for prayers, the poor relics of Byzantine wall-painting, the cheap incense, the droning chant that seemed to have put God to sleep. Coolness, kindness, a few birds. Absolute isolation from the world.

Herbs

It is hard to know when monks first became devoted to the sick and the dying, and to be collectors of herbs and makers of medicines, including liqueurs and elixirs, from Chartreuse to Buckfast Tonic Wine. It seems to belong naturally to their role as wise men, readers of books deeply embedded in their rural surroundings. It also belongs, of course, to their benevolence. The good old hermit encountered in the forest is an impressively benevolent force even in the romances of the late Middle Ages. Shakespeare knew the legendary hermitage of Guy of Warwick, not far from Stratford. Monks must naturally have been herb-gatherers, and the knowledge of written books about herbs as the materials of medicine descends through them from the Greeks and Romans, and from the Arabs, to the Western Renaissance. When Buddhist monks first came to China, they founded hospitals there. Monks ran hospitals in the West, and the type of charity to be found at the old London Charterhouse, Ewelme in Oxfordshire and Kirby Hall in Yorkshire, which catered for children in a school and old people in a cloister in one and the same institution, was surely based on monastic examples.

The existence of a class of permanently sick people, which is so swelling today, is largely a product of scientific medicine. In the early Middle Ages, you either recovered or you died, or you survived as a cripple. Old age did not last long. The monasteries responded to the problem of the sick as it began to increase with the growth of population and the organization of medicine. But their role as herb-gatherers is fascinating from the beginning. Of course there were local variations, and specialized charities. They knew more about snake-bite and scorpion sting at Monte Cassino. Chartreuse is the product of Alpine meadows and Buckfast Tonic Wine is less strong. All the same, one of the best bee-keepers and breeders in Europe is a very old monk at Buckfast to this day. The dogs of the Hospice of St Bernard were bred to dig travellers out of snow-drifts.

We can be precise about the knowledge of herbs. The greatest surviving illustrated manuscript of herbs and flowers was written for the daughter of a late Roman emperor. The text is that of Dioscorides, a Greek writer on the materials of medicine, and the wonderful botanical drawings in it probably derive from a Greek painter. It was brought west at the Renaissance from Constantinople, and is now in Vienna; it is extremely fragile, but at least it has been fully photographed. From this kind of ancient illustrated book a long succession of lesser manuscripts derive, mostly in monasteries.

The most popular author was Apuleius Barbarus, who wrote in the fifth century. I can still remember almost by heart his paragraph on strawberries, which I cannot have read for nearly thirty years. The illustrations were formalized as they were copied from one manuscript to another until they lost contact with nature. But when Apuleius was first printed, still being thought a useful book, apparently by a Sicilian in the entourage of Pope Sixtus IV, he took his copy from a ninth-century manuscript at Monte Cassino. The illustrations became woodcuts; the plants are just recognizable and very beautiful. The picture of each plant shows the beast whose bite or sting the plant was supposed to cure, including a vivid scorpion and an odious-looking snake. One of the earliest recorded illustrated books was a kind of identity chart of dangerous snakes, illustrating an Alexandrian Greek text in hexameter verses. Even some scenes of torture in later manuscripts derive from ancient illustrated medical manuscripts misunderstood. The hanged man in the Tarot card pack is an example.

The most popular plant book in the late Middle Ages was written by Bartholomew the Englishman, a monk of some kind who was a pupil of the Dominican Albert the Great in the thirteenth century, who as we have seen was one of the few medieval teachers who has the right to be called an empirical scientist. The same age saw the first direct observations of nature, of birds in particular, to be made in the West since the fall of Rome. Accurate botanical drawing had to wait for the full Renaissance. Bartholomew's book *On the properties of things* was printed in 1470, and then twenty-five more times before 1501. It included an alphabetic catalogue of trees and herbs, and some theoretical comments deriving from the work *On plants* which in the thirteenth century was attributed to Aristotle.

The history of monkish medicine does not end there, of course. The Director of Kew Gardens attended a conference in Athens in 1934. Naturally he went plant-hunting in what was then the unspoiled countryside. There he encountered a monk, an official plant-gatherer with the resounding title of Hieromonachobotanos. The monk carried a huge black bag which he said contained four folio manuscript volumes copied from Dioscorides. By consulting these great tomes, he identified the plants as he discovered them. One must add that in an old-fashioned Mediterranean culture herbs are important. Country women still gather their salads, and you can buy sixteen varieties of wild tisane, mountain tea, in the market at Chania in Crete, the commonest being mountain sage which every housewife brews. The varieties of honey are innumerable, and most monasteries keep bees.

In the matter of herbs one can observe an interesting balance between the learning of monasteries, the benevolence of monks, and the natural culture of the countryside in which the monasteries grew up.

Ground Plans

The Sankt Gallen plan is an ideal blueprint for a monastery. It was made at Reichenau, on an island in the Bodensee, the western arm of Lake Constance, and sent to the Abbot Gozbert at Sankt Gallen in about AD 820 give or take a little. The plan was carefully and beautifully drawn to a scale of two and a half feet (Carolingian feet) to each of the squares of the grid, much the same as the surveyors' grids of the Roman Empire. It is not at all impossible that whoever drew up this fine plan was imitating the procedure of Roman town plans. He was not surveying any single, particular monastery, though scholars have often wondered whether they sensed the influence of just such a plan. It has been suggested that the Sankt Gallen plan was a prototype for the new movement of monastic reform and reorganization which can be dated to just the same few years. It certainly has an interesting relationship to that movement, ideal if not practical.

Even apart from its square-based grid, and appealing Romanesque clarity of shape, which certainly constitute a revival of antiquity or a survival of Roman values, the Sankt Gallen plan confirms the rootedness of later monastic architecture and therefore much of the monastic way of life, in the best traditions of ancient Rome. There is something wilfully conservative about medieval monasteries, with their archives and Latinity, and the small gardens sprouting between buildings, the monumental temples, the cold colonnades. The dying Empire sprouted tiny communities and groups of dissident hermits, but the monastic ideals of the Sankt Gallen plan would have been intelligible, architecturally speaking, to Hadrian. The cloister in the shadow of the cruciform abbey, as of Tennysonian elms that "layed their dark arms around the field", is a colonnaded

Roman forum, overshadowed by basilica and temple, a formalized Greek agora or marketplace. Even England has yielded up excellent Roman examples of this plan. It remains remotely possible, of course, that the monastic cloister goes back not to the Forum, but through Pacomius in Upper Egypt to the parade ground, the Roman barrack square.

At Oxford and at Cambridge, the abbey with its cloister and common buildings became the college with its chapel and its courts or quadrangles. At the Reformation the word cloister became more or less taboo. The Cambridge word "court" is taken from secular architecture, and the Oxford word "quadrangle" appears to be an invention, at first maybe a joke. Shakespeare uses it, and so does Gregory Martin, the Fellow of St John's who wrote most of the Douay Bible, having previously taught Shakespeare's Stratford schoolmaster at Oxford, so it appears from their dates. Tom Quad at Christ Church, Oxford, was planned by Wolsey, finished by Henry VIII, and glorified by Wren. It had sprouted cloisters but they never grew; that must surely have something to do with fashion. Quadrangles were in and cloisters were out. Where the lawns are now in colleges, fruit trees used to grow; the last traditional college grove in a quadrangle belonged, I think, to Brasenose and survived until the eighteenth century. Fruit trees and rough grass and a few sheep might be a great improvement on the bald magnificence of later centuries.

In the Sankt Gallen plan, east is at the top. The rising sun shines first into the great east windows of the abbey churches. John Donne on his monument in St Paul's still looks east "in expectation to behold him whose name is Orient". To have east at the top of a church plan or of an ancient temple plan or tomb-temple plan would seem natural. I am not certain why north is at the top of our maps unless it has something to do with the North star. But the construction of an entire monastery in gridded squares in an oblong enclosure like a sheet of parchment, on the exact east–west axis of the Sankt Gallen plan, square within square, can seldom have been precisely carried out. Roman camps were planned like that, but they were designed to be built overnight by drill movements, by a legion. Monks were less disciplined, and their buildings were not as swiftly constructed. They are more like vast, rambling encampments or organic growths, with cloister leading to court, and archway to colonnade, year by year for miles. They ramble like Pliny's villa, where the remotest door was never opened; it was found to have taken root into the ground, and put out fresh leaves.

All the same, the heart of monastic architecture is already visible in the Sankt Gallen plan. The cloister is its central square, protected from the north by the vast bulk of the abbey and shaded from the south by the monastic refectory. If Cardinal Wolsey's scheme had been carried out and the Christ Church College Chapel built, that would have been the system in Tom Quad. The Sankt Gallen plan goes so far as to provide for animals' quarters, as well as noviceship, abbot's house, guest house, infirmary, cemetery and so on. These are separate buildings, rather geometrically organized than architecturally unified. They are laid out like allotments. No doubt it was winter and east wind that crowded together the monastic buildings in so many cases, and unified them as a single protective organism.

The abbey church in the plan has a great apse at the west end as well as the eastern end; indeed, it is almost symmetrical. A similar emphasis is still to be seen in the splendid western end of Reichenau. It has been explained as a particular German tradition, something to do with processions perhaps, and the way in which the elaborate meanings of the liturgy were spatially articulated in the ninth century. At a great eleventh-century monastery like Jumièges, the west end is only an elaborate entrance. The west end of medieval St Paul's was rebuilt by Charles I as a piece of royal theatre. So it is at least worth noticing that the basilica with an apse at each end is a classical Roman convention; one can see it, for example, in the basilica of the forum of Severus at Leptis Magna. In many ways, the Sankt Gallen plan remains a puzzle.

Language

The monastic intellectual world of the West has always been based on Latin, and in Orthodox countries on elaborate and archaic Greek, not on the vernacular languages. If it is true as scholars believe that Benedict wrote his Rule in extremely rustic Latin, it was swiftly polished to the normal dull lustre, and the monks always fed on a rich diet of Augustine and a variety of similar writings, while to each successive generation the accepted Latin must have been more of an effort. A large part of the famous monastic studies must have been spent in mastering the language, and, at least until the spread of literacy and calligraphy from about the tenth century, in learning the liturgy by heart. Priests and choir-monks could read and speak Latin when few laymen could do so; hence their usefulness as diplomats or officials of the state.

But the difficulty persisted. A Norman abbot could impose the discipline of silence by forbidding English and allowing only Latin or French. Even in the very late Middle Ages, the poet Gower was unusual in being able to write verses in all three of those languages with equal skill. An English bishop at Rome was laughed almost out of court in the twelfth century for his rough and unready Latinity. The Irish monks treasured their manuscripts of early Irish poetry, and wrote some of their own. The Lindisfarne monks were reproved about their enthusiasm for Danish epic poetry just before the Vikings came in 793. The story of the martyrdom of Edmund in Anglo-Saxon reached Aelfric, who wrote it down, from a monk of Fleury, who had it from Dunstan. Caedmon's Hymn, the earliest Christian poem in Germanic verse-form, was recorded in writing, and so was Bede's dying poem. "The Bible should be read in the refectory", wrote Alcuin to Lindisfarne, "and the reader heard and not the harper."

His attack was directed against pagan heroes, but essentially vernacular heroes. The heroes of classical Latin literature were more acceptable, because they were useful for learning Latin, and now and then one reads of some exception being made to the general damnation of pagans, so that Trajan, or Virgil, or whoever it might be, did not have to languish in hell. "Beowulf" and the other great manuscripts of Anglo-Saxon poetry appear to have been written down in Wessex monasteries in the tenth century, though traces of dialect suggest a more northerly origin for the poetry itself. One of these manuscripts has been in Vercelli in Italy since the thirteenth century.

The survival of vernacular poetry and legend in monasteries in spite of Latin dominance is natural enough; in fact one is rather reassured to hear that it happened. The transmission of classical Latin through monastic manuscripts is notorious, though one must remember that the growth of the great monastic libraries was closely connected with the patronage of such figures as Charlemagne and his successors: it was a deliberate royal rather than a deliberate monastic policy. Individual monastic scholars were sometimes apologetic. William of Malmesbury wrote two couplets of Latin verse in a twelfth-century volume of minor Roman writers, written out under his direction. "With this book William wasted his time, adding these small matters to his studies, which for your mind's sake you may run through reader, since when great things weigh heavy lesser things give pleasure."

It is interesting in this light to assess the creativity of monasteries by what they produced in Latin, Latin being their dominant culture. Their theological writings are so vast as to be uncontrollable by anything less than a lifework. At the great periods of monastic explosion in Western Europe, among the early Cistercians, the early friars, and the first Western monks of all, there are moments of attractive brilliance in theology, and something similar occurs among the Orthodox. One might tentatively suggest the same about Buddhist monasticism. Monastic historians can be skilful and fascinating in any language, but they are never in advance of the general culture of their age. Even the great Maurist scholars of the seventeenth century belonged to a general European movement; they were as much the inheritors of the Renaissance as Voltaire was.

Latin poetry shows a somewhat different pattern. Helen Waddell thought the great age of the Latin lyric was 1150–1250, and she ended her anthology with the Arundel manuscript, written in the late fourteenth century, with a poem composed around AD 1200. I would personally be inclined to put the flowering a little earlier. I have certainly never seen any Latin poetry of the Renaissance or later of any merit at all written by monks. Did Latin lose its cultural dominance then, even inside the monastery walls? Today, and at any time since about 1650, a monastic poet would write in his own vernacular. Julian of Norwich, the writer of *The Cloud of Unknowing*, and even the ecstatic Richard Rolle wrote far more sharply in late medieval English than any English monk in Latin in their day. When Latin lost its general, secular dominance, the Latin-dominated monastic culture lost its intellectual teeth. The opposition of the Counter-Reformation and neo-scholasticism to the modern world is only a later stage of the same process.

Yet while Latin poetry flourished in the monasteries, it had a freshness and strangeness, and the monasteries were alive. No one then thought them absurdly reactionary. Today, in those religious houses where secular literature is read at all, the good monk is the one who reads the football pages and the middlebrow classics. He may even read Helen Waddell's *Medieval Latin Lyrics*, because they are charming and remote. She does give examples of words or lines scored out by monastic readers from the most pagan poems. But there is no doubt that secular, unbaptized culture flourished within monastic environments, at least as a sub-culture, as part of literature and part of music. The Archpoet was no monk, though he frequented cloisters and died about 1165 in a monastery. The ninth-century poem about the Abbot of Angers is not monastic, though it is clear that some monks enjoyed its very broad anti-biblical humour. Latin poets of the eighth and ninth centuries in and around monasteries were less inhibited than those who followed them. My personal favourites are the Carolingians, the Blessed Notker Bibulus, so called because the other monks fled and left him at the mercy of some Vikings, with whom he had a happy drinking session, and perhaps Walafrid Strabo, who composed a lengthy sub-Virgilian poem about gardening.

Great poetry in Latin is rare in the Middle Ages; it is never a monastic monopoly, and most of it occurs early, when Latin is still two-thirds alive. Even the *Dies Irae* is the reworking of an old theme, the amazing language of it being based on verse adaptations of Jerome's Latin vulgate version of the minor prophet Zephaniah. A long tradition of wonderful Latin lyrics descends in the same way from Jerome's version of the Song of Songs. They shift from secular to religious meaning and back in a way that only such an original could admit, down to the time of John of the Cross. It is fascinating that a similar tradition with the same basis exists in medieval Hebrew, though the two perhaps had little contact. The last great Latin poetry ever written, with some very few neoclassic exceptions, was not charming pagan lyrics like the *Carmina Burana*, which are refreshing in their way, but the brilliant hymns of Thomas Aquinas and the still more amazing monastic poetry of Abelard. Thomas has the majestic wingbeat of a flight of swans, but Abelard soars on the lightest of wings. This is his hymn for St John, written for Héloïse in her convent.

Coelo celsius	Heavenlier than heaven
volans aquila	the eagle flying
ad dominici	even to the musteries
sinus abdita	of the Lord's breast
nidi condidit	has made a dwelling-place
habitacula	and built his nest.
Solis intuens	He sees the shining
illic radios	of the sun there
summo iubare	in supreme light
beatissimos	shining most blest,
visum reficit,	and feeds his eyes
pascit oculos	his sight refreshed.

Ex substantia	Out of the substance
solis ignea	of sunfire
calor prodiens	heat that proceeds
et lux genita	and generated light
oblectamina	offers absolute
praebet maxima	of delight.

This same disgraced poet and luminous reasoner was not above humorous verses in his hymns. His hymn to St Paul refers to that apostle as "untamed rhinoceros God set to plough, to smash the clods of the low lands". *Hic rhinoceros est indomitus quem ad aratrum ligans Dominus glebas vallium frangit protinus.* Among his more famous hymns is "O Quanta qualia", on the joys of heaven. One has the impression of a genuine mystic in spite of a few stumbles, or at least of the closest a powerful poet could come to that condition. He branches out far beyond monasteries, yet his hymn to St John is the pure product of monastic Latin culture, and expresses as well as Bernard could do the driving force of monastic vocation in their lifetimes. The rhino came from Job.

Books

Since when have scholars been so interested in monastic libraries? In the fifteenth-century Italian Renaissance? Perhaps very much earlier, because already in the eighth century, when the Northumbrian monasteries were collecting and copying books, the copies were in demand all over Europe. Boniface wrote to the Abbess Eadburh for the Epistles of Peter in letters of gold, and the Abbot of Wearmouth for the works of Bede. The gifts missionaries sent in return for books were such things as Byzantine silk embroidery for wrapping the relics of the saints. Most of the books that monastic libraries had in the high Middle Ages came to them as gifts, and the search from one monastery to another for rare or useful authors never ceased. When the intellectual world that came to centre on universities broke away from monastic dominance after a struggle in the twelfth century in which some of the great teaching masters became monks, and Bernard of Clairvaux and the woolly-witted William of Thierry fought hard against non-monastic teachers, the search for books continued both outside and inside the abbey walls.

Kings and their courtiers were more book-hungry than monastic scholars. Such a minor potentate as Lord Berkely in the fourteenth century supported John Trevisa, an old Oxford scholar, Fellow of Exeter and Queen's, to write him books and make him translations, and perhaps to paint the walls of his church. Trevisa was a pleasant poet and a fine prose writer. In Italy there were similar and far greater figures at the papal court and the court of Florence: and that is how the Renaissance began, the great monastic book-hunt which ended in the ransacking of some libraries being a part of it. As books had flowed into Northumberland and into Charlemagne's France, they still flowed into the great intellectual centres that generated new books, but these were no longer monastic. The libraries of the Conventi Soppressi are an important part of the Laurentian Library at Florence.

Books were produced in the high Middle Ages not only by monks but by monasteries acting as patrons to professional artists, and both kinds of book were of great and elaborate beauty. It therefore becomes an interesting question when the monks ceased to care about the beauty and even the contents of their books. Art styles in the decline of the Middle Ages and earlier were international. The illumination of books was over-sweet and mechanical before the invention of printing. The intellectual decline of monasteries was patchy and complicated; it was not a single uniform movement; monastery by monastery, as the Church reacted to the Reformation and became in fact intellectually reactionary, the lights went out. The magnificent revival of monastic learning and intellectual edge in seventeenth-century France was simply part of a European movement, a spirit that was stirring outside the walls.

The Oxford University library's best building is still called Duke Humfrey's library after Humfrey Duke of Gloucester. It contains many monastic manuscripts, but not only were they nearly all looted from their first homes at the Reformation, but the Oxford library itself was looted at the same time, to get rid of wicked papistical texts. It had to be refounded, which is why it is named after Thomas Bodley, a later Protestant merchant and book-collector. But as late as the seventeenth century John Aubrey saw monastic manuscripts from Malmesbury being used to block a hole in a beer barrel. In my lifetime I have often seen them used as lampshades. They turn up as wrappings round eighteenth-century estate papers. You can buy scrapbooks of monastic illuminations and stray leaves of monastic books. So it is hardly surprising that the keenest intellectual book-raiders have scoured the libraries of the Levant, and the more enterprising archaeologists have dismantled and carried home what they could of the monastic relics of Buddhism. In England they have systematically excavated the graves of the monastic dead in order to rob the graves of their tiny religious treasures.

In England the Reformation was so thorough that no monastic libraries survived, though some cathedral books did. But from about 1425 onwards, the hunt was for stray manuscripts of the pagan classics, for the Bible and for illuminated manuscripts. Interest in most of the contents of most monastic libraries was far less. It is amazing what classical and unlikely writers the monastic libraries of Europe turned out to contain. We know of a monk in an Italian monastery attached to Cluny, called the Abbey of Farfa, who was issued Livy for his private Lenten reading in the mid eleventh century. Another monk in the same year was given Josephus and a third had a History of the English, though the other sixty monks had more improving theological works. But as the recovery of the pagan classics became more and more intense, the monastic libraries of Europe were exhausted, and hungry Western eyes turned to the Levant. It will be remembered, after all, that Tischendorff found the most thrilling of all Greek Bible manuscripts under an old teapot in the desert monastery of Sinai. It was his reward for getting there first, but we now know that he by no means penetrated all the treasures of the Sinai library.

It is probably best to let a book-hunter speak in his own words. Robert Curzon travelled in search of manuscripts in the eighteen-thirties, and published his *Visits to the Monasteries in the Levant* in 1849. A hundred years later it was still a cult book among the more educated kind of Oxford undergraduate. Curzon had been a secretary to the British Ambassador to the Sublime Porte (Turkey) and had already travelled in wild places as a book-hunter in Italy. He was rather an enterprising sprig of diplomacy than a great scholar. Here he is at the Meteora, the tall rocks on which the monks nest like vultures above the Thessalian plain.

> After looking over the books on the shelves, the librarian, an old grey-bearded monk, opened a great chest in which things belonging to the church were kept; and here I found ten or twelve manuscripts of the Gospels, all of the eleventh or twelfth century. They were upon vellum, and all, except one, were small quartos; but this one was a large quarto, and one of the most beautiful manuscripts of its kind I have met with anywhere. In many respects it resembled the Codex Ebnerianus in the Bodleian Library in Oxford. It was ornamented with miniatures of the same kind as those in that splendid volume, but they were more numerous and in a good style of art; it was, in fact, as richly ornamented as a Romish missal, and was in excellent preservation, except one miniature at the beginning, which had been partially smeared over by the wet finger of some ancient sloven. Another volume of the Gospels, in a very small, clear hand, bound in a kind of silver filigree of the same date as the book, also excited my admiration. Those who take an interest in literary antiquities of this class are aware of the great rarity of an ornamental binding in a Byzantine manuscript. This must doubtless have been the pocket volume of some royal personage. To my great joy the librarian allowed me to take these two books to the room of the agomenos, who agreed to sell them to me for I forget how many pieces of gold, which I counted out to him immediately, and which he seemed to

pocket with the sincerest satisfaction. Never was any one
more welcome to his money, though I left myself but little
to pay the expenses of my journey back to Corfu. Such books
as these would be treasures in the finest national collection
in Europe.

But did he get away with the books? He did not. The librarian
demanded half the money, the Abbot refused, they bargained, the
Abbot offered too little. So the librarian raised the whole community
of monks, like a swarm of very angry bees, to demand equal shares
all round. The Abbot stood on his dignity, the money was paid
back, and Curzon had to unpack his baggage. He had one last look
at these wonderful volumes, which now he thought were like
Norman stained glass, and left them with the sun glinting on the
pretty silver. Everyone concerned was disappointed, and "the old
librarian, after walking up and down once or twice with his hands
behind his back in gloomy silence, retreated to a hole where he lived,
near the library". In just such a hole Tischendorff discovered the
Codex Sinaiticus under the teapot. Curzon's servants offered to
storm the monastery and get him his books, but he refused.

It is worth underlining some episodes of this sad story. Curzon
likes treasures, and prefers them beautiful and rich. His heart beats
to the pride of possession; he had not intended to resell the books.
He seems little interested in their contents, and less than expert at
reading Greek writing, in both cases probably less so than the
despised monks. His nonchalant reference to the Codex Ebnerianus
at Oxford means probably that it was on public exhibition, and
more famous in the eighteen-thirties than it is today. His interest
in binding is meritorious, but more curiosity about the inside of
books would be more meritorious still. The idea of "the pocket
volume of some royal personage" is important to him. He is extremely romantic in his slightly vulgar way, and a poor bargainer who
shows his passion where the monks conceal theirs. He is in every
way in contrast to the monks, and one ends up liking them more
than him, though one also likes his cheerful bodyguard who are
willing to blow everyone's head off, *parce que le coup de fusil leur*

flatte les oreilles, as a contemporary of Curzon's remarked of the people of Naples.

This kind of thing ended badly for us all. I was once on the island of Patmos working in the monastery library. I worked in a hut on the roof, among a team of palaeographers from Athens who were making a record of the library. They were Byzantinists, a trade that scarcely existed in Curzon's time. As Greeks they had vehement feelings about the plundering of Greek monastic collections by English book-hunters. I wish I had known then as I know now that the first and worst and most interesting altogether of this tribe was a Renaissance Italian called Cyriaco of Ancona. The Byzantinists were charming, and we made common cause. I got the books I wanted through an extremely old monk librarian and his equally old friend. When I asked for one particularly ancient and priceless volume he banged it and banged it until clouds of dust filled the room. It was in fact the wrong book, but I hastily accepted it for fear it might disintegrate. I was given good marks for this, because it was the works of a Father of the Church they really respected, Gregory perhaps, and they were thrilled that the young foreigner was reading him.

When I left I tried to give these two nice old men a tip. They had already refused a contribution to the monastery. I said vaguely they could use it as they chose. They went away and muttered; then they came back and said No, No, No, Popopopopop. They were very old and I was young, and therefore I should keep this money because I was still capable of enjoying myself, and they were not. So that was that, and at the end of my last delicious day I stood waiting for the island ferry to Athens, which was going to take all night. The ferry was late because a storm had got up, but I nearly missed it altogether, because at the very last moment of all I was hauled into the police station and searched. One of the younger and more ambitious monks, whom I must say I had always thought a nasty bit of work, had told the police I was probably buying manuscripts from the library in secret. I was not accused of stealing. But as I had taken a lot of notes, many of them in Greek, and the police did not believe any foreigner could write in Greek, speaking it being suspicious enough, I had a lot of explaining to do. The Greek monastic system had its revenge on Curzon in the end, though I dare say my journey home, stormy as it was, must have been luxurious compared to his.

Modern monastic libraries at their best are like almost any small institutional library in Europe. Some of them are grand, some homely, and they all contain books rare in the outside world, so that for certain subjects scholars have to consult them. The library of Port Royal survived the ruin of that great foundation and can still be consulted in Paris. It is still looked after by old Jansenist families. The Jesuit libraries are often rich in the literature of obscure or dusty controversies, though few of them have a continuous history. Part of the old library of the Palermo Jesuits survives in secular ownership next door to their house. This is because of the suppression of the order for a time at the end of the eighteenth century. The Jesuits are not quite monks, but from the library point of view they are much the same. Old institutions accumulate books, and the best libraries are well housed, little consulted, because handling is the ruination of books, and very, very old. At the end of the Middle Ages the book collections of the great European monasteries must have been magnificent.

Today the edition of some voluminous Father of the Church is usually an international, always a co-operative task, and in some of these there are monks who take part. Benedictine Solesmes has established a proper style and standard for printed Gregorian chant, and made a vast contribution to the history of music, more or less on its own. There are more learned periodicals than I have been able to master devoted by monks to monastic history. But the sharp edge of advance in most learned fields, even when they border on the nature and history of monasteries, lies elsewhere, and there are even questions of the attribution of quite important writings that no one inside the monasteries has got round to settling. Jobs like that would once have been done by guesswork in a cloister by one clever old man, but today they demand a patience and a range of research that a monastery can seldom muster. All the same, within these limits there are still splendidly learned monks. As scholars and as human beings they are exemplary. But a monastic library is no longer sufficient to nourish a scholarly lifetime, and they depend inevitably on other, non-monastic institutions. Yet at the decline of the Roman Empire, most of the bookish knowledge available in Europe would have been more available to monks than to anyone else.

Why not admit that one sometimes longs for the conditions of an old monastic copyist, with his long, slow mastery of just a little? It is partly the unclutteredness of their minds which is enviable, but then also the objective demands and rhythms of calligraphy, and the satisfying result of a durable book. The earliest paper ever used in the West was recently discovered in the monastery of St Catherine at Sinai, and both paper and papyrus are easier to use and rather less enduring than vellum, which medieval monks used, and which covers the gap between papyrus and paper. There is one other argument which favours that stone age of reading: certain books are not much read unless monks read them. They are a neglected part of our culture, an abandoned part. The mystical writers of the Middle Ages and the imaginative theologians have been abandoned among the mass of rubbish that surrounds them; they are redis-covered only by monks to this day. It was Thomas Merton, not my favourite monastic author, who led me to the commentaries of Gregory. I came across Bernard on the Song of Songs rather by mistake. Whenever in some great cultural conflict one side wins and one loses, the dominating side always loses something torn away and left with the defeated. The monks were losers, maybe still are losers, but they retain secrets the rest of us envy, and the secrets are to be found in their libraries.

Art

No one is surprised that Buddhist art when it arose, several centuries after the Buddha, whose religion was one of abstinence, withdrawal, morality and contemplation, was recognizably one thing from Afghanistan to China. Of course when one inspects it in more detail, great differences appear, and an abundant variety. The narrative art that appears as ornament on the stupas and spreads through the great cave sanctuaries, monasteries of a kind, and the wayside shrines of Central Asia explored by Sir Aurel Stein, turns out to have Greek and Roman sources, among others. The same communication through travelling monks occurs in the West. Benet Biscop introduced into Northumbria the Roman techniques of cement flooring with embedded bits of pottery, and the Levantine art of coloured glass windows. At the same time the books of customs and rules of different monastic houses spread like hedge fires.

The religious wall-paintings of the Cappadocian monks in the high Middle Ages are a world apart from the magnificent arts of Byzantium. They are stronger, warmer, more brutally realistic, and clear and forceful in narrative. But similar paintings of the eleventh and twelfth centuries have been discovered in the Latmos Caves, near that most magical of all monastic sites where the pagan Moon loved sleeping Endymion, from which the refugee monks set out to find the monastery of Patmos. Gervase Matthew found similar paintings at Hosios Loukas near Delphi, in the crypt of the church, and in Cyprus. He is not alone in seeing a close connection with Greek religious paintings in south Italy. The interest of all this is not art historical for my purposes, but it lies in the idea that monastic painters moved about.

But objects move more easily than people; I have seen in the small museum at Ghazni in Afghanistan a stone relief that appears to have been copied for an Islamic ruler from a Byzantine embroidery. The splendid tonsured monk embracing the feet of an angel on the stone shaft of a cross at Dewsbury is a Northumbrian stone sculpture based on a Byzantine original which cannot have been so heavy. I do not really think it is an angel at all, but a winged John the Baptist in the Byzantine convention of the time. Angels do not normally have beards, even in Northumbria. The Buddhists used pattern books, and one can find misunderstandings of pictures in their stone-carving. There is one based on an illustration of the Trojan wooden horse. In the West, images were certainly transferred from one medium to another, and the Latin verses that went with them confused and crumbled into prose. However things happened, there is no doubt at all that an international community of images travelled very swiftly between Western monasteries as it did among the Buddhists. The Carolingian paintings in the "lower crypts", that is the crypt, at Saint Germain d'Auxerre were not an isolated phenomenon as their surviving fragments might now appear to be. "Lower crypts", incidentally, means any vaulted cellar, and "upper crypts" means any vaulted building above ground. The winter ambulatory of Timur Lang at Isphahan is an "upper crypt"; so is the winter ambulatory at Fountains. At Constantinople even the cisterns were vaulted as soon as they were dug. The earliest Christian crypt may be that of the tomb of Peter at Rome. The crypt of the Holy Sepulchre at Jerusalem is probably fifth-century.

Consider the Buddhist cave sanctuaries in the same light. The magnificent Ajanta caves in India date from the second century before Christ, and Indian cave monasteries are the origin of Buddhist ones. The caves of Bamyan in Afghanistan as they survive today, in their latest, most elaborate form, honeycomb the cliff face, and mysterious stairways in the darkness of the rock lead up to the heads of gigantic stone Buddhas that dominate the valley. Innumerable tiny cells, all decorated and some of them carved into lotus ceilings, must have been places of meditation. We have written evidence of enormous numbers of monks flocking into Bamyan; the cave sanctuary was monastic. A similar pattern is repeated all the way to China. Maichishan in northwest China is another and perhaps more beautiful Bamyan.

Maichishan looks like a holy mountain, the mystical axis of the universe. We know that the Buddhists thought so in the sixth century AD. For the pure idea of such a mountain one should consult the marvellous model of one in a gallery near the very top of the Victoria and Albert Museum. No one knows whether Maichishan was an ancient "Taoist" holy mountain before the Buddhists got there; it is perfectly possible, and it is what happened elsewhere. Cave dwellings in the soft rock and cave sanctuaries among them were older than Buddhism in northern China. So is the excavation of rock-tombs with a shrine for worship at the entrance. There is a Buddhist burial of that kind at Chiating with a seated Buddha at the entrance from the second or third century AD. At least thirteen Buddhist cave sanctuaries have been recorded in an area west and southwest of Peking, roughly between Szechwan and the Alashan desert. One surmises that there may be many more.

Buddhism spread and its shrines blossomed in the early fifth century under a Hunnish ruler called Meny-sun who was patron to an Indian Buddhist monk called Dharmaksema, for whom he collected a fine and famous library. The foundation of Maichishan was the climax of a Buddhist religious movement in northern China. The founder was the monk T'an-hung, who arrived soon after AD 420. Pupils gathered round him. In 425 or so another monk arrived with another hundred disciples. In the end they are said to have had three hundred between them. But conquest by the Wei Tartars and persecution of Buddhists brought the second monk to his death at the Emperor's hands, and the first to suicide by burning in Cochin China in about 455. The village people "saw him with a golden body riding very swiftly eastward on a golden deer". Surely with very few changes this could all be the story of the foundation of a southern French monastery within a hundred years of the same date. (It would be later in France.)

In 452 the wicked Emperor died and Buddhism revived with

renewed patronage. The Tartars set up a new capital city not far from Maichishan, and we have inscribed evidence of their patronage. Caves were extended and Buddhas commissioned. Local pilgrims were attracted. Once again we might be talking about somewhere like Saint-Germain d'Auxerre. Landslide, earthquake and political and military upheaval played their part in the history of Maichishan as similar events did in the history of European sanctuaries. In the mid sixth century a commander-in-chief commissioned the niches of six Buddhas in memory of his father, with sculpture and painted decoration. In France it would have been a splendid stone tomb in a mortuary chapel. A poet wrote about the old gentleman's memorial in much the same terms as Walafrid Strabo or any other monastic Latin poet might have done.

> He had a path like a ladder to the clouds built in the south face of the rock, and the niches of the Seven Buddhas carved as a temple-offering for the repose of his father's soul. This work was like a carving of sandalwood, a sculpture of river-jade, it shone like the full moon . . . even in this wild place now there are halls where the Law is taught. As on the Fragrant Mountains, here also we can meditate before the divine images.

I suppose I must admit that the Chinese poet is better than Walafrid Strabo and his like, but not much better.

In 581 the Emperor decreed a temple at the foot of every holy mountain in China. In his day the Buddhist monks in China numbered 230,000, and their temples and shrines were recorded as 3,792. Forty-two sets of the Tripitaka, the pilgrim story, were copied out, thousands of books were repaired, and 106,580 holy images were set up. It works out at about five images per monk, and about seventy monks per temple or shrine. The only incredible thing about it at first sight is the swarm of dozing images, but some of them may have been small and simple. At Maichishan at that time the activity was prodigious. But by AD 759 we hear that "In the remoter shrines few monks remain: the narrow paths climb high through wilderness: musk deer sleep among rocks and bamboo groves, and cockatoos peck at the golden peach. Streams trickle down among the paths." An Irish poet might have written like that at any time.

There is no point in continuing the story in detail. China suffered its suppression of the monasteries through imperial avarice in the ninth century, its many invasions, and its peasants' revolts in 1208 and 1224. In that year the monks were expelled and their grain-stores looted. The next year the army suppressed the rebellion and looted the monastery again. Maichishan decayed slowly, with a small revival in the sixteenth century. It was rediscovered by archaeologists retreating from the Japanese. This is the only point in the entire history at which one feels the West might have done a bit better. But at least in 1958 the monastery of Maichishan still existed. "The wall had many stones with inscriptions embedded in it; it dated back to the Wei (Tartar) period. One of the early monks found a very precious herb which he sent to the Emperor . . . The Empress E-Fo lived there as a nun . . . We were told that her apartments were probably on the site of the upper wing where we lived . . ." The European analogies, in Greece, for example, are numerous. The only permanent inhabitants were the curator of the caves and an old monk of about eighty.

The beauty of Maichishan is utterly beyond expectation. It can best be studied in the photographs in Michael Sullivan's *Cave Temples of Maichishan* (1969), which are by Dominique Darbois. The hill is small, rocky and squared, the shape of a castle pudding, perhaps a hundred or two hundred feet high, and tufted with trees. The Buddhas are of many styles, sizes and periods, some of them of great beauty, others of fearful grimness, as the statues might be in an English cathedral of great antiquity. But Maichishan is more magnificently decorated. Its statuary is very peaceful and very powerful. The Bodhisattva on the left wall of cave 100, which belongs to the Wei period, stands comparison with the archaic Korai of the Athenian Akropolis. More of the statues than one can number are in their own way equally impressive. Small wonder that the monastery at the foot of the hill lasted so long. As an aid to contemplation, such a place would act on the mind at least as powerfully as the liturgy.

In our day monasteries all over the world are likely to fall into disuse. The same constitutional weakness finds them out. They once transmitted book-learning, medical care and public morality, but they find it hard to survive in a literate, numerate world. Once there were five hundred Carthusian houses, now there are scarcely five hundred Carthusian monks. I seldom hear my colleagues discuss religious sculpture of any kind; even in Greek art their interest is largely erotic. I have never met any young man on fire to set out for Maichishan. The international style of art peddled and admired in modern monasteries and convents is horrible beyond expression, though that bleak-faced old seagull, Our Lady of Reading, has her clients still, I am glad to see, in Westminster Cathedral, and the wealthier religious institutions sometimes worship before antiques. When Nijinsky won the Derby, Campion Hall at Oxford was given a fine medieval statue of the Virgin to celebrate the win.

National styles prevail in monasteries, as well as international styles. The Germans like starkness and petrified drama, the Italians are pleased with shabby beauty, the rags and tatters of the past. The Americans favour a fearful type of neo-Gothic, which I take to be Irish American in origin. You would never imagine the sweetness of the people from the curious buildings they live in. In England the style is mostly that of public schools, very undistinguished indeed, and with certain touches of what Pevsner discussing Harrow calls "hearty and confident gloom". Amazing exceptions do occur, as in the fine Dominican chapel in Oxford, and Matisse's chapel, another Dominican building. But in the past the builders of monasteries were the most interesting architects of their time in Europe at least, and we shall never see that again. Nor is it likely that the visual arts will have any future renaissance engendered by monks. Perhaps there are not enough monks left to engender anything. The old man at Maichishan would be a hundred and ten by now.

If it is true that many Western monastic sites are physically impressive and the sparse ornaments recovered from them very pure in quality (but they were never as splendid as Maichishan), that is a question of patronage. At Lindisfarne on the Northumbrian coast, for instance, with its wilder hermit rocks and the dominating bulk of Bamburgh Castle, or at Ynys Seiriol on Anglesey, a hermit community which like Lindisfarne is little more now than an archaeological site, the natural setting is humanly very attractive indeed. Lindisfarne was rich in arts at one time, but not on the grand scale, and it did not survive long enough to accumulate great monuments. It was a big wooden church at first, with small study cells or prayer cells and a common dormitory and guest house. Ynys Seiriol was a church and a line of rectangular drystone hermit-ages. Nothing recovered from Northumbrian monastic sites except a few stone animals in their naive way, and a few fragments of metalwork, meets the high aesthetic and technical standards of Maichishan. Indeed, there is nowhere in the world to equal it, neither in Afghanistan nor in the Indian subcontinent, including Ceylon. In Europe one would have to appeal to the pre-Christian past.

Monks appear to be a product of monotheism; the few exceptions to this rule can all be disputed, and it is interesting that although there are no Jewish monasteries, there was something very similar at the time of the Dead Sea Scrolls. I think we can safely say that Christ knew no monks. The Jewish Rabinnic schools had rather an Islamic than a Western monastic character. But it must be admitted that Buddhist shrines in and around Afghanistan were strangely transformed in the course of time. At the late stage of the Buddhist shrine at Ghazni excavated by the Italians in the late sixties and early seventies, the central cult object, or at least the object on top of the hill, was an Indian mother goddess seated on an elephant. It was a shrine, perhaps, but not a monastery. Or the monks vanished and the last saffron robe was gone, but the shrine survived in use and the local ruler refurbished it.

I am no great expert at Zen monasticism, but it is clear to me that Zen, as a philosophy of life, has very pure origins and diffuses easily by continual transformations until it becomes something else in California. Perhaps the last of the swift distributions of thought, feeling and style of which I have been speaking is the diffusion of Zen. In the quarrel between religious and secular, the spirit was left somehow to the monks, like mouldering snow before an avalanche. There followed a revolt, within the secular world and in secular terms, of the individual against the institution. It is evident that the spirit speaks to the individual, and its values would not as easily be sought for in the ruinous neo-Gothic shades of institutional religion. The appeal of Zen Buddhism, in so far as it was genuine, which measured by such a scale as the poetry of Gary Snyder it clearly must have been, was that of the least institutional religion in the world.

Thomas Merton on the Asian expedition on which he died was in conference with Eastern mystical teachers whom he respected greatly, and I assume rightly. There seems little doubt that they were after the same thing, and by similar methods. John Harvey, in a review that dealt with Cistercian architecture, remarked about Sufism that "This is not to say that the Cistercians were less Christian than their contemporaries but that they tended (doubtless unconsciously) to go beyond Christianity." Bernard would vehemently disagree with this, and it does seem to involve putting a limit to Christianity that Christians have never acknowledged. Yet there is something in it. What monks have in common all over the world is an important *arcanum*, an element of their identity which outsiders can only suspect.

Part 5

The Everyday Life
of Monks

Conditions of Life

The best modern account of life in a monastery is Patrick Leigh Fermor's *A Time to Keep Silence*; it is written from an outsider's or a guest's point of view, and its monasteries are mostly French, but it captures the atmosphere and the other essentials perfectly. From an insider's point of view we have only the writings of Thomas Merton, in most ways an extremely untypical American Trappist. Normally, if a monk perseveres in his monastery, he finds his routine becomes a second nature, difficult to write about. Nuns are more sharp-eyed, but they are normally too busy to write about daily life. It is not always safe to rely on ex-monks or ex-nuns, nor are they usually much concerned with those details of daily life that interest outsiders.

These details differ from Order to Order and from place to place more than one would think. The great formal refectory of one house with its pulpit for public Latin reading and the abbot washing the hands of guests in a silver basin corresponds to a rather jolly country house breakfast room in another giving on to a lawn. In France the public reading used to be *recto tono*, chanted rather than read, but all on one note, for fear of dramatic displays and self-indulgences by the reader. If the reader made a mistake the senior monk would interrupt, *repetet*, let him repeat. It is fortunately quite hard to tell the finer points of Latin pronunciation *recto tono*, so the reader could usually guess what his mistake was. In England the interruptions were more direct. According to the kind of monastery, the book might be more or less serious. Nowadays it is mostly in the vernacular, or entirely so, which leaves a very open field. An unpopular book will be very unpopular indeed. I recollect Harold Nicolson on good manners as a low point. Pastor's *Lives of the Popes* is so deadly that it was treated as a punishment suitable for Lent. On one occasion we were all so fed up with it that someone stole the volume and hid it. It was about Volume 19. At the next meal they started page one of Volume 20, with the clear intention of going on until Volume 53 unless Volume 19 reappeared. This would not have happened in a well-regulated monastery.

It was Benedict who introduced the vow of stability to Western monastic life, which is perhaps its greatest difference from Eastern monkish life. The novice vows to live and die, unless otherwise commanded, in the particular monastery that he has entered. Hence routine, hence the slow rhythms, the established community of all ages, the special traditions, the care over electing abbots, the subtle mitigations and obstacles to tyrannical government. And hence the famous Benedictine peace. Friars belong more to an Order than to one particular friary, though they do chant the office when at home. Very few nuns take a vow of stability, but in my experience they move about less than men. Nuns are more catlike, monks are more doglike. It is perfectly possible even today for a boy in a monastic school to enter that same monastery and just stay there for ever, though he may perhaps attend university courses as a young man. He will do that in a house of his Order, and without neglecting the office. In my day at Oxford the young Benedictines used to have to get up and leave, all in a body as if at some hidden signal, half-way through any evening meeting they attended.

In the past, the conditions of secular society had important implications for the monks and nuns. It is not by chance that the only three religious books in English in the late Middle Ages which can be called masterpieces all seem to have been read by women, or at least two of them. It is because Latin was not demanded of women; they were lucky if they could read. These three books are the *Ancrene Rule*, a rule book for hermits, *The Cloud of Unknowing*, a treatise on mysticism and mystical union with God, and the *Revelations* of Juliana of Norwich, who was a hermit, or more precisely an anchoress, a hermit in a cell built on to a church. Even Westminster Abbey had one. Women were not allowed to live in a cave. It is clear also that the agricultural basis of society has taken an enormous part in forming the way of life of monks, not only with labour in the fields, but with the kind of authority and work in administering estates that monastic officials did, and the kind of solitude a monastery might enjoy, the kind of patronage they might expect. Today, religious superiors have lunch with their investment brokers, or they speak to them on the telephone. As landlords and feudal lords in the late Middle Ages they were constantly going to law, and sometimes to court.

Benedict's experiment had failed by its great success, and reform after reform came to seem overdue. Reform of various explosive kinds is something monastic communities have always generated. It does not need to depend on a great figure or a serious intellectual movement. Indeed, monastic life is a constant process of self-reform and community reform. A monastery, like a monk, can only go forwards or backwards; it can never stay the same. That is the saddest thing one must say about monasteries. The routine is a mirage, not an oasis. Sometimes reform means a walk-out; the Benedictines walked out of York to become Cistercians in the wilder parts of Yorkshire. (Only the nuns reached the very wildest parts, and only the monastic sheep and their poor shepherd got to Malham moor, though a hermit lived up there summer and winter in the seventh century.)

The decadent seventeenth-century Abbé de Rancé, Richelieu's godson and the queen's darling as a child, had an *amitié amoureuse* with a duchess twice his age. She died, and by some horrible accident he saw her head, decapitated by an undertaker. He sold and resigned his possessions and his sinecures, and retired to an abbey he owned called La Trappe, a gloomy spot. There he and his valet set themselves up as monks. He threw out the few inhabitants, installed some severe Cistercians, and set up a way of life of unique ferocity. His reform transformed the Cistercian order, who are now called Trappists. The only survivors of the "unreformed" order are monks in a few Central European monasteries that he was unable to reach, and some nuns whom he never noticed, based in Belgium. They have schools in England and mission schools in Africa and Japan. They are very nice nuns indeed; my sister is one. But it would be fair to say that in the course of centuries, particularly this one, they have lost much of their peculiarity. Their rule is to drink the drink of the country, and being mostly French they used to get wine, but now they get tea. I do not think the ones in Africa have taken to African food or drink yet.

One of the strangest reforms was what happened on Caldey. It was an Anglican Benedictine community of monks set up on Caldey Island in 1896. The island is wonderfully wild, and lies off the coast of Pembrokeshire. I have never landed there, though I once sailed close enough to see the seabirds, which include puffins and guillemots and even wilder, stranger birds. This monastery lasted seventeen years. Then all but two of the monks became Roman Catholics in 1913 and built themselves a new monastery at Prinknash on the steep edge of the Cotswolds, hidden in woods not far from Birdlip. The Pope let them go on wearing the white habits they adopted in 1895, but they had to take new vows. Heath Robinson's son was one of these monks, and Heath Robinson drew a memorable cartoon of the monastic building process. So there they still are, fewer of them now. They used to have the biggest and most beautiful bull I had ever seen. We used to go there by bicycle from Oxfordshire on pilgrimage to see this bull. An oblate of Caldey, one of the few survivors whom the others deserted, went off and founded Nashdom, which in 1981 was just over half the size of Prinknash.

It is not the only monastery in the Church of England. There are also Anglican convents. The oldest is the Society of the Holy Trinity, now at Ascot, founded in 1845, which sent sisters to the Crimea with Florence Nightingale. I doubt whether much in their daily life is distinguishable from a Roman Catholic order; their rule is the Rule of Benedict. Much earlier Anglicans made serious attempts at monasticism, under difficult conditions. Nicholas Ferrar's community at Little Gidding which nourished Crashaw and loved George Herbert was virtually a monastery, and it is not surprising that Charles I sought comfort there. My own opinion is that Eton, with its collegiate structure, was very like an abbey with an abbey school in the early seventeenth century, with its fellows in residence, and a strong interest in theology and mysticism. I have seen the Eton edition of Chrysostom in the library of a small monastery in Greece. Sir Henry Wotton translated a love poem by Horace into a dialogue of God and the soul that reads like John of the Cross. John Aubrey went to Eton and found John Hales reading the *Imitation of Christ*. Another fellow became a missionary priest. Everyone went to chapel, of course. What they lacked was a vow of stability, and political stability as well. It is all too long to argue here.

One of the monastic routines we know most about is that of Cluny, the medieval associated abbeys, not quite a separate Order, of the latest Benedictine pattern before the Cistercians at the very beginning of the high Middle Ages. We know it because these monasteries eagerly collected one another's custom books, to know how things were done at the mother house or in other famous houses. Benedict does not cover every detail of life and there are questions of interpretation, of the letter versus the spirit, and so on. Benedict himself envisaged a government by deans, with every ten monks having a dean of their own, a specially intimate superior, but this system scarcely survived. Its enfeebled tail is the Oxbridge system of deans of discipline, or in America "dean of men" and faculty dean. Custom books do not cover every detail either. They are the accumulated decisions of superiors about matters they wished to regulate. They are most full on the subject of liturgy, the principal work of the monks. But they can also descend to such bizarre details as the prohibition of playing hoops in Magdalen cloisters, of feeding or annoying the deer in the park at Roehampton, of playing musical instruments in certain places. In my noviceship private singing practice had to take place "behind the woodpile", but the pig-sties beyond that were out of bounds.

One of the best eleventh-century Cluniac custom books is really a report by a monk of Farfa in Italy of the customs of the mother house, but we also possess one by Ulrich of Cluny written for the

175

Abbot of Hirsau in 1075, to satisfy the holy man's anxieties. I will not discuss the office and liturgy in great detail, because the subject is vast, the variations infinite, and their interest specialized. In religious life a liturgy bore, who is always in command of the minutest and obscurest regulations, is worse than a canon law bore. But even the general standard is exacting. Not everyone could pick out the proper office of the day when regulations conflict, but everyone would know every movement of every role, and every word of many prayers, in the principal parts of the office and the liturgy. Only the very old and mad make mistakes. It is generally agreed that the coronation of Elizabeth II was conducted with great magnificence and propriety, yet I remember a sense of involuntary shock at seeing important officials having to be told what to do. With bishops, on the other hand, who often have ideas of their own which must be followed, it is more a question of wondering what they are going to do next and acting accordingly.

The Cluny monks slept in one undivided dormitory with the boys of the Abbey school. They wore nearly all of their clothes nearly all the time, though they took off their cowls, their deep hoods, in order to sleep. They seldom got clean clothes and very seldom bathed. They shaved on the vigils of great feasts, all at once in a line, passing the bowl and the razor from hand to hand. They wore their cowls when they went to wash or for other purposes of nature, in order to preserve their privacy. They rose between two and three in the morning, just at the time that shepherds begin to move in the south to this day, in order for their flocks to catch the refreshing morning dew. The bell would be tolled. A clock was rare for long after 1075, and it had no bell; time was therefore inexact by our standards. The monks had to be in choir when the bell stopped tolling, a system that still prevails in colleges and schools and parish churches all over England. One of the most impressive of all sights is the assembly of Carthusians for the night office, each one from his separate hermitage, the deeply cowled figures, the tiny lights coming together. The office started with preliminary prayers, a sort of religious throat-clearing before the serious work. Some of these prayers became in the late Middle Ages intolerably verbose and rhetorically eloquent. Reform movements usually cut them back.

The first office was matins, which had nine nocturns, consisting of chanted psalms, responses, lessons and collects. The little wooden shelf on which one could half-sit, called a misericorde, is still to be seen in numerous abbey churches. A churchwardenish monk went round with a lamp, which he waved gently in front of any monk who fell asleep. This office lasted until dawn, and it is fair to say that this was the principal task of the entire monastic day. Lesser offices, private prayer, some manual work, and some reading and meditation punctuated the rest of the time. Seasonal changes made things worse in Lent and tougher in summer, when sleeping in all one's clothes was particularly irksome. The first Mass came early, after private prayer, and the ordained priests said their Masses then, but later in the morning High Mass was celebrated with great ceremony. At Cluny, the schoolboys under their master attended the night office.

Cluny kept extra offices, that of the dead, and that of All Saints, which were miniature versions of the office of the day, in addition to the normal office. They also chanted some extra psalms. This increased burden is to be found in liturgical books as late as the Renaissance. The office was work, it was among other things an endurance test. Old Carthusians say that the one thing one never gets used to is the lack of sleep. Small wonder that the patrons and even the peasants in the fields were grateful to the monks for their perpetual prayers. Patrick Leigh Fermor found that attitude in France, and Richard Hughes found it on a remote Greek island. It amazed me when I was first told by an undergraduate friend from a monastic school that the purpose of all priests was to pray for the living and the dead. I do not now think he was wrong.

On great feasts church and cloister were decorated, as churches still are. The monks were woken for night office by the pealing of all bells. The office had fine music; the Advent antiphons were already thrilling before Christmas, and the mournful church manoeuvres of Holy Week were already touched here and there with a foretaste of Easter. That liturgy has recently been devastated by reformers in an attempt to impose clearer meaning on it. Yet it had its rhythm, and one grew into the rhythm. Even small variations in the liturgy have great interest in a routine life. The dramatic variations of Christmas and Easter and Pentecost were thrilling. One looked forward for weeks to the changes of colour of vestments and hangings, the splash of red for the descent of the Holy Ghost, and the two days in the year, mid-Lent and mid-Advent, when the priest wore rose-pink.

In the days of Cluny, the monks sat every day in tiers around their chapter house after Mass, with the abbot, or the prior if the house was a priory, something less than an abbey, in the presiding chair. A chapter of the rule was read aloud, the rule not being a set of regulations like the custom book, but a nourishing document that enunciated principles. Most of the older monks would know it more or less by heart from constant repetition. The abbot or prior then gave an address, a cross between sermon and instruction, but without rhetoric on the whole. Then business was discussed. Rule-breakers confessed their faults and were given penances. Ulrich of Cluny says the boys had a "chapter" of their own, at which they were stripped and beaten with a willow cane for offences of behaviour, sleeping in chapel or bad chanting. There were about a hundred choir monks at Cluny. They had plenty of servants, and as many as fifty of them did administrative work while the rest read and wrote. It was the same at Canterbury. Ulrich of Cluny says that the manual work done by monks amounted to no more than shelling the new beans, baking bread, or weeding the garden. On the days when that was done, the Abbot shortened the chapter meeting and announced manual labour. The boys led a procession and psalms were sung. After the weeding the procession came back to the chapter house. It does not sound as if they weeded for long, but village work in the fields in the last century began and ended almost as formally.

The monks did not get much to eat, and some quarrels are

recorded in the later Middle Ages, and numerous abuses. They were hungry. In summer they had a mid-day dinner and a supper at night, in winter dinner in the late afternoon and a snack at bedtime. They went to bed early by our standards. Silence was important, but there was a repertory of finger-signs in which in my own recollection one could even be eloquent or make jokes. They ate no meat at all at Cluny, but they did eat fish and they did drink milk. Fowl were what one might call a grey area; in some places and times, they were held not to be meat; a curious controversy about whether the barnacle goose was fowl or fish lasted the length of the Middle Ages. The barnacle goose is a winter migrant. It spends summer in Britain only in the extreme north of Skye. I cannot imagine why the monks were so interested in the idea of eating this beautiful sea-bird, unless they were very hungry indeed.

Probably the most disturbing single factor in the lives of settled Benedictine monks was the constant noise of hammering and the voices of the builders, with one loud reverberation in every hundred years when a bit of the monastery buildings fell down. As institutions they showed restless persistence in building and rebuilding, perhaps because of their vow of stability.

Some Anthropological Notes

Asceticism lies at the root of the monastic movement everywhere. A kind of self-punishment, a kind of discipline, underlies all the spiritual liberations and contemplation of the one God, and withdrawal from the world into peace. There is little doubt that the earliest monks were Indian ascetics, or that from Indian monks all other Asian monks arose. They were mendicants and therefore wanderers. The low status of women, which is, of course, exaggerated by men self-bound to chastity, meant that there were no nuns, and it was unthinkable to have religious orders of holy beggar-women. The same problem recurred in the West in the early history of the Franciscans, at a time when European women had lost the higher status they once had. Franciscan nuns were forced by the Pope to possess property held in common, because it was unthinkable for women to beg.

The status of religious women in the West has varied widely with the alterations in society. The Anglo-Saxons thought it normal to have a double community, one of men and one of women, who were as literate as the men, with a single abbot or abbess and one church. But in disturbed times, which were not long in coming, convents as we now call them were more vulnerable than monasteries, and few survived. Today about sixty out of the ninety English RC Benedictine nuns live in the abbey of Stanbrook, but there are more women's orders in existence in Britain than anyone can count, each with its own rules and customs and its own founder, sainted or likely to be sainted when the order can afford the expensive process. They run schools and hospitals, care for the dying, rehabilitate whores, look after priests and bishops, care for the poor, or consume their lives in adoration.

The most formidably learned nuns are probably those at Stanbrook. They nearly all have degrees, and each of them specializes in her chosen Father of the Church. The English translation of their liturgy horrified many of them, because it abolished the fine distinctions of Latin prose style between the lessons from various Fathers read out in the office. I can remember that change with awe, since it happened soon after I was first obliged to recite the office every day. Not being a monk, I never had to chant it in choir, but those who did had to accept English, and the most horrible botched and bourgeois sub-episcopal English, as communities. Had I been a monk I would surely have run away at that time. The older ladies at Stanbrook whose lives had always had a sweet formality, a play-acting of hierarchy with nun bowing to nun and so on, very appropriate to a life of silence and liturgy, were greatly disturbed when all such innocent distinctions and performances were abolished by Rome at about the same time. Still, I am pleased to say that at least the bowing has come back, and they have probably got used to the English by now.

More modern orders which spend more time on their work, as teachers or hospital sisters, had less time for the stately pace of ritual, and working nuns are often let off from large parts of the office. When they are cut off for a time, they long for it. The office is essentially an induced habit of chanted communal prayer. It has a rhythm of its own, and if your mind should wander that rhythm still controls it. The progression of the chanting is communal and inexorable, as if it had an objective reality independent of the individuals who are in fact doing it. It goes deep into the nature of monastic life, because it is almost purely mechanical. The majestic pace of the office in a great abbey seizes the mind, but it is still too fast for the monks to consider every word they utter. In lesser institutions, particularly convents, the chant whizzes along like the buzzing of melodious gnats.

Those who are forced to read the office alone usually keep up a good pace, though I have known several priests bound to this daily task who felt the need to go slowly and savour the words, so that they found it impossible to get through their task for the day. Before the office was shortened in recent times, it used to take three hours for a clergyman sound in wind and limb. There was then a law that reading must involve some minimal movement of the mouth, so one could watch the old men striding up and down with their prayer books, silently gabbling. The reason for the rule is simply that God must have his due, and the eye might slide too swiftly over the page, as indeed it often does. As late as the days of Jerome, people thought he had a magic art because he could read with his mouth shut, without mouthing the words as children still do. The Church has always distrusted intellectuals, and the office was meant to be chanted or recited. It was verbal prayer, not mental prayer.

And yet music, regularized music, makes it both. The rhythm

carries the voice and the voice carries the mind. The chanted office wonderfully concentrates thoughts and feelings. There is no doubt at all that for experienced monks the set forms of the office and the liturgy liberate, they do not constrain. They are their own kind of contemplative prayer, and music is essential to them, as it is in a cruder and briefer way in hymn singing. One of the critical moments of religious life is the time when verbal prayer begins to drop away, and wordless attention takes over, for longer or shorter periods. This is a common experience, but sometimes a religious novice is anxious in case they may not be praying at all: novices being subject to scrupulous anxiety of many kinds. The attention and inattention combined in the experience of the chanted office, and its fine musical control, with the variation imposed by cantors, lessons, repeated responses and alterations of psalm-tone, and the sense of the slow underlying movement of day and night and season, perfectly bypass this problem. The paradox is that the dutiful chanting of words is in fact wordless prayer. At least I hazard this conjecture.

The theory is that by possessing the whole body and soul, thoughts and feelings of the monks and nuns, the office spills over into their whole day, making their entire lives a liturgy. Unfortunately man is not so constituted, and in their active moments monks do not always behave like contemplatives. This is as true of contemplative Buddhist monks as it was of medieval Western monks. Women being nicer than men, the nuns tend to spend themselves in endless charitable endeavours, so that the work itself sets their pace. The psychological difference from most men's orders is great. But if we take some rural abbey like Stanbrook as an example, instead of a suburban school or a city hospital, it becomes obvious that the Rule of Benedict, seriously observed to the exclusion of whatever would be intrusive, is at least as suitable for women as it is for men. Some temperaments prefer smaller institutions. It is an important question to what degree nuns are willing, so to speak, to live in one another's pockets, and what kind of work they can do. The worst of all religious penances is community life: it is not the penances of religion, which are private, but its communal pleasures which are hard to tolerate. In women's orders there is sometimes a grue-some aping of natural relationships. "Sister" is bad enough, but the wearing of wedding rings as brides of Christ, with other such play, and calling the Superior "Mother", would not suit everyone. Of course "Father" is as bad, but at least that is a title almost drained of meaning in the Roman Church. "Brother" I have always found odious because it is not meant.

It embodies a sharp distinction of class. You say Brother to a lay brother, that is, a religious who works manually and will never be ordained or have any important part in the chanted office. He will never be a religious superior. Lay brothers were, traditionally, assumed to be illiterate. In the Jesuit order in England, you graduate from Brother so and so to Mister as soon as you leave the noviceship and wear clerical clothes, and you are addressed as Father. I had a friend who was addressed once as Father, and once as Sonny, the first day he appeared in London dressed as a clergyman. In Italian, I was instructed to use the polite third person to priests, "thou" to contemporaries, and "you" to lay brothers, "you" in Italian not being as polite as it can be in French. In England I was once at lunch in the clergy house at Manchester when they were discussing Father Martindale. Someone said he was an extraordinary man, equally good with dukes and whores or boilermen. Up spoke a brother from the bottom of the table, rather mildly under the circumstances, since his job was to stoke Victorian church boilers. "I don't think whores and boilermen are quite the same, Father." He was sternly rebuked by the Superior. "Now, now, Brother, we'll have no socialism here." The story is not typical, of course, but there were such old men, and I have hated them passionately for forty years.

Do you think nothing so wicked would happen among nuns? You are mistaken, but I blush to print the stories. Or in a real, old-fashioned monastery? Read the life of Thomas Merton, and observe how one at least of the Cistercian lay brothers hated him, and ask yourself why: it was not a mere matter of temperament. It is more painless to record incidents from the remoter past: for instance, how the medieval monasteries treated their serfs. It is not really good enough to say that they treated them as other feudal lords did. The treatment was flatly contrary to every human and every Christian principle. The serfs were taxed by their lord if they married off a child of either sex, or sold an animal, or died, and arrested if they left their village or worked for someone else. For the lord they worked for nothing. Those impositions were imposed by force, and often illegally so, on those who were in fact freeborn. The phrase *nativus de sanguine*, "native of this place by descent" was used as equivalent to serf. There were also slaves, though I know nothing about monastic slaves; I assume that lay brothers were invented to fill their place.

The Cistercians not only had lay brothers but servants and serfs as well, and their famous architecture after their pioneering days was an international style constructed by professional builders. John Harvey, reviewing a book on this subject, *Architecture of Solitude* by Peter Fergusson, suggested that it derived almost directly from Seljuk Turkish architecture, and it is tempting to believe so. He also thought its inward-looking and contemplative quality was oddly similar to the spirit of contemporary Sufism. I had already found this a fascinating thought, but I am unable to develop it and know of no concrete way to verify it. Undoubtedly mysticism did move westward with Arab influence, but it also existed in the West already. The spirit blows where it chooses.

We do know a little about the buildings. The more geometrical that building techniques became, the more the abbeys needed to be professionally built. In the twelfth century, the precise alignment of architecture and fine, flat, ashlar construction that recalls fifth-century Athens suddenly appeared in France. They owe their existence to the revolutionary impact of Euclid's geometry, which came to Europe from Arab sources before 1120. The first buildings of the new Cistercian foundations were wooden huts that the monks and their lay brothers built themselves. I have met Jesuits proud of having built churches and schools in Africa, physically, with their hands. But the second stage soon follows. The monastery or mission flourishes, and then you use professional builders who impose an international style. The Cistercians maintained a particular severity by annual visitations of the abbey buildings, but ineffectively in the end. Bernard had a strong prejudice against towers; the tower at Fountains is still standing, but it was not built until about 1500.

In the labour shortage in the English countryside in the late fourteenth century that followed the plague, the monks did not behave well. The monasteries had come to depend, as they were bound to do short of begging in the streets as the friars did, on permanent pools of traditional labourers, and the condition of villeins and serfs and *nativi de sanguine* suited them very well. They would never have flourished without its existence. It is the dark side of their moon. It is as child labour is to the agricultural and industrial revolutions of the eighteenth century. We hear of the Abbot of Meaux in the East Riding of Yorkshire removing his villeins from the jobs they had with relatively rich peasants, to come and cultivate the Abbey's land for nothing. The Abbot of Pipewell in Northamptonshire exerted similar force. They were both successful at law, which is how we know about the disputes. The Prior of Durham demanded labour not only from labourers and workmen, but all cottagers and all tenants without crops of their own who had sublet their land or failed to sow it. The agent and the forester were ordered to prevent any such people leaving their village. The Abbot of Evesham charged a tenant twenty shillings and eight pence for permission to employ his own brother. The Abbot of Pershore hired out a man, *nativus de sanguine*, to work for six years at three shillings and sixpence a year. The land nexus flowed easily into a money nexus. So that in the abbeys they should go on chanting.

Sometimes the monks went too far. John Mole was Cellarer of St Albans Abbey, that is a sort of bursar, from 1354 to 1373. If labour was not forthcoming after the plague, then a rent in money was charged. Durham raised its rents, the Abbot of Eynsham increased his income, and Ramsey Abbey increased the burden on its tenants with the same excuse. John Mole of St Albans went so far as to demand arrears of rent. These arrears were not only difficult but really impossible to pay except in very good times indeed. Even today it is usual for farmers to be heavily in debt to the bank; in the Middle Ages a tenant farmer could not, of course, mortgage his land. St Albans became an extremely unpopular institution, though as a centre of artistic patronage and liturgy and intellectual activity it might seem to have attained great brilliance. Facts like these lie behind the Peasants' Revolt, the Reformation, and the suppression of the English monasteries. They do not, of course, detract from the innocence of an old nun in Yorkshire weaving wool in Swaledale, or an old monk in his choir with his mind on heaven.

Contemplatives

Monks of all religions are addicted to the contemplation of God, an undistracted absorption interpreted as a union with God. It was not invented by monks, though it may have been by hermits, but one is unlikely to encounter it often in the secular world, which is distracted, and plagued by fears and desires and everyday anxieties. Contemplation was known to Socrates and to the earliest Indian mystics. It appears to go beyond any dogmatic framework, but careful frameworks of discipline and dogma have been constructed around it by the Sufi mystics, by Buddhist teachers, and in a thornier entanglement than the others by the Roman Church, which has an entire branch of theology devoted to it. But love laughs at locksmiths, and facts come before the explanation of facts. The Curé d'Ars was asked by one of his worried parishioners how one should approach God. Straight, he replied, like a cannon-ball. Not that cannon-balls do, in fact, go straight; nature abhors straight lines in the flight of cannon-balls as in everything else, perhaps even in the contemplation of God.

It is not a necessary part of the monastic calling in the West to wish to attain the state of contemplation, but the hankering is very common. Probably unless it is suppressed for some reason of prudence, dogmatic rectitude or false humility, it may be a universal human velleity. The theologians of the high Middle Ages made it the definition of heaven, and therefore in some sense the vocation of all mankind. It recurs in quite different cultures with opposing dogmas, but it always involves discipline and asceticism, and forms of prayer that are apparently deadly boring – in Greece the simple repetition of a phrase or the name of Jesus, in Tibet the repetition of a phrase which may even be wound round and round mechanically while the contemplative silently contemplates, and so on. It can be aided by gentle drumming, but it is not a state of hypnosis, and Aldous Huxley's fantasy that it could be simulated or stimulated by drugs was a disaster that has few disciples left.

Contemplation, according to the contemplatives, is not an attainment like climbing a mountain, or a special mixture of genius and circumstance like producing a work of art, and it is not a natural, involuntary process like dreaming a fine dream. Some contemplatives have, in fact, been subject to involuntary transports of various kinds, but so have mad people. Mysticism undoubtedly has psychophysical phenomena, such as the stigmata, which have been studied and finely distinguished and to some degree explained. The contemplatives we are forced to call genuine and authentic, words one would more freely use of a poem but must use in this case with quasi-scientific care, set little store by these exotic phenomena. John of the Cross appears to have performed a miracle for a joke. Someone wanted asparagus, and he produced it ready to eat. That, of course, has nothing to do with contemplation, only with exotic phenomena.

I feel it is best to follow the dull, old-fashioned writers on this subject, and neither the thrilling Latin writers nor the modern textbooks. What most monks attain to in the course of their lives, or are given as a grace, if you take the extremely cautious line of some Catholic theologians that contemplation is a special gift of God and by no means a general vocation, since it breaks their normal rules about the soul, is what Bossuet, who seems to have invented this expression, called the prayer of simplicity, or the prayer of simple regard. This is common enough among religious people inside or outside monasteries. Theologians say that to be properly called contemplation it has to last for some time, but, as one would expect, they argue about how long a time. They all agree that they are not talking about those strange transporting moments we have all known, whatever we believe about them, but about something habitual and sustained. Serious contemplatives have the ability, as Dom Cuthbert Butler pointed out in 1922, in his excellent and solid *Western Mysticism*, to keep some crucial area of their minds gazing at God while they carry on business. It would be easy to parody his view, but those who have known contemplatives would agree that it is more or less true.

Meditation, an exercise recommended by most monks and religious teachers, fixes itself on images or on phrases; it is discursive. Contemplation dispenses with images. "The imperfect contemplative spirit commonly in his business is full of multiplicity", but when it prays "easily getteth an unity and simplicity in soul, which is an emptying or casting out of all images of creatures", and "easily findeth and treateth with the unity and simplicity of God, which immediately appeareth unto him". On the other hand, "The prayer of the contemplative life is a quiet, affective prayer of the heart alone." Butler is quoting a much older monastic author. The transition from meditation to contemplation is most of what John of the Cross means by the night of the senses. That is the title of the first book of his prose treatise, *The Dark Night of the Soul*. One may hazard the guess that few monks or priests get far beyond it, though I have been told and believe that more nuns do. Pleasure in prayer and in meditative thought withers away, and the contemplatives find themselves much simplified, but also more vulnerable. This experience and this teaching seem to be common to different religions, and to different theories.

The belief to which so many monks down the ages must have devoted their lives is mystical rather than dogmatic. It is an odd fact that when the tree was shaken under Henry VIII the monks who held on to their branch were contemplatives. They were too deeply embedded in their mysterious relationship with God to give way about a point of dogma, a point of theology, even though almost every professional theologian did give way. It is not theology that saves. Neither is it liturgy. The one way in which the English monks were impeccable at the time of their dissolution was in the chanting of their office and the solemn performance of all their rituals. Contemplative prayer is in a way invulnerable, it enters into the identity. One does not need to suppose that God was as it were opened to the minds of these Carthusians like a chink of light. The point is rather their absolute fixity of purpose, which was intellectual as much as it was voluntary. Something similar has been suggested by those who have most successfully resisted torture in our life-times. Of those I know, none was to my knowledge a contemplative. It is a matter of the deepest sense of identity. Whether monks have sought out such a depth intuitively in order to endure their lives is to be doubted. They thought of it as a normal fruit of their lives. Some medieval writers have thought of their monastery as an earthly paradise restored, and there are monks alive today who would agree.

Augustine was not a monk, though his writings were an inspiration and a model for monks for many centuries, and the idea that a bishop (which he was) should be or should live like a monk derives from him. He thought contemplation was the highest act of the soul, an opinion that goes back to Plato and beyond, and that "if we steadfastly hold to the course that God commands us" we shall somehow arrive at it. He makes the deliberate point that this was not an intellectual attainment but open to simple, secular Christians. He was enthusiastic about the wonderful lives of Egyptian hermits who "enjoy conversation with God and are most blessed in the contemplation of his beauty, which cannot be perceived save by the intellect of the holy", but he did not think they had the monopoly. One may find his phrases about the hermits stilted and even rhetorical, though that is too often true of his style to have special significance here. Gregory the Great makes the same point that monks have no monopoly, nor did they invent contemplation. But it would be fair to say that in the later Middle Ages interest in contemplation was more and more confined to professional religious figures, monks, nuns and hermits. The interesting mystical writings of fourteenth-century England were transmitted almost exclusively through the Carthusians, which is why they mostly remained in manuscript until a hundred years ago or less.

It is as if by turning their backs on the world and breeding a culture of their own the monks had taken away with them an important part of God, and locked it up in monasteries. The works of John of the Cross were printed in Spain in 1630, after elaborate negotiations with the Inquisition, when he was a canonized saint. It is likely enough that had the Reformation in England happened otherwise, had the division of cultures not taken place at all, the old English mystical writings like *The Cloud of Unknowing* would have been printed in England in the same age, perhaps after elaborate negotiations with Archbishop Laud. Dom Cuthbert Butler was Abbot of Downside, and the purpose of his work was to reverse the catastrophe. Unfortunately he would not be popular reading even in a more religious period than ours. Within thirty years his book was dusty and neglected. All the same, though it is not certain, it appears likely that mysticism and monasticism have been entangled in the Western as in most Eastern traditions for a very long time. It looks as if Cassian brought them both to Europe from the Egyptian desert. The fifth-century writer called Pseudo-Dionysius, an important influence in the later Middle Ages, gave to mysticism a further blast of Eastern light.

Lawrence of Arabia, no contemplative but a tricky and dangerously charismatic personality, tells an Arabian story somewhere that I think illuminates the lives of monks, in the way that only a metaphor can do. It is about the ideal palace of some rich and exquisite Arab sheikh. Its courtyard was full of fountains and flowers, and it had seven great rooms. He describes the styles and furniture of these rooms, which were wonderful, but I have forgotten them. He went from room to room, every one of them quite different from the last, with different hangings and surprising views. The last and most valued room of all was painted white, and quite bare, and it was open to the desert. Perhaps some readers, suspicious of the idea of the contemplation of God, will accept this as a metaphor for the mystical component in human beings.

John of the Cross was a friar, which I take to be a monk of a kind. He was brought up virtually as an orphan in Castile in the forties and fifties of the fifteenth century. He was probably from a Jewish family recently "converted", but it is likely enough that he never knew it. The culture of his place and time had many Islamic and Jewish elements, but it was of course Catholic. He was discovered to be scholarly at the hospital for advanced cases of syphilis at Medina, where he was working, and was offered a chaplaincy there, but at twenty-one he became a Carmelite. He studied at Salamanca in a small Carmelite college; one of the professors was Luis de Leon, who soon afterwards spent five years in the prisons of the Inquisition for translating the Song of Songs into Spanish. In 1567 he was ordained priest and went home to say his first Mass at Medina. There he met Teresa of Avila, a Carmelite nun who was directing a reform of the women's branch of the Order and anxious to interest the men. She was just founding her second house. He agreed to devote his life to the reform movement. The Carmelites had originally been hermits in community, but as refugees they had turned into mendicant friars. Teresa wanted to go back to the rules of 1247, severe poverty, enclosure, prayer and fasting. The reform prospered, but men are nastier about these things than women, and John ended up in a monastic prison, an abandoned medieval lavatory, where he might well have mouldered until he died. He was taken out two or three times a week to be flogged in front of the conservative monks, insulted and mocked. It is not a nice story. But in that prison he became a mystic of absolute authenticity, and also one of the greatest poets in European history. Then, luckily for literature, he escaped, so that we have his writings: both the poems and songs in which mysticism is hidden and encoded, much as the Sufis encoded it, and the prose works in which he explained himself.

The prison was in Toledo. He seems to have been inspired by a lovesong sung in the street outside. "Of love I die, dear love what shall I do? Die alas, die."

> Muérome de amores
> Carillo. ¿Qué haré?
> – Que tu mueras alahé.

But much of his own poetry was purely Renaissance in tone, its technique was Italian, and very much of it was based on the long-established ambiguities of the Song of Songs. It was common for nuns and priests to exchange poems on a single devout theme, and Teresa and John had done so; now the nuns copied and sang his songs, some of which did take the form of popular songs. At his best, John of the Cross is so musical as to be untranslatable into our language, full of lightness and fire. "My beloved the mountains, The woods in the solitary valleys, The foreign islands, The echoing rivers, The whisper of the amorous airs . . ."

> Mi Amado, las montañas,
> los valles solitarios nemorosos,
> las insulas extrañas,
> los rios sonorosos,
> el silbo de los aires nemorosos.

Another stanza speaks of Night tranquillized, kindling before dawn, silent music, sounding solitude, the supper of refreshment and eros. How different from the dry treatises of the theologians; scholasticism flourished in the Arab world as it did in Europe. But mysticism encoded speaks more directly, with greater intensity and greater purity. In June 1591 at the age of forty-nine John of the Cross was deprived of office in the reformed Order and in December he died. The reform was successful though, and the reformed Order exists today. It is clear from the fuller version published some years ago of the autobiography of Thérèse of Lisieux, a nineteenth-century French saint, that the Carmelites can still produce canonizable saints, but also that all is not always sweetness and light inside convent walls. Teresa of Avila, the friend of John of the Cross, remarked that it was not surprising God had so few friends, considering the way he treated them. Teresa's own writings are so fine and vivid that they express their time and place almost too well. We know more about her reform of the Carmelites than about most monastic reforms, but the story is utterly personal because of her being such a good writer in her plain way. As a footnote to this story it is amusing to remember that nuns were forbidden by Charlemagne to sing songs about love of any kind.

Teresa had died at sixty-seven a few years before John of the Cross. She was as much a mystic as he was; she had been a nun since she was twenty, at first in a big, fairly relaxed community. It was the habit of private, mental prayer, intensifying after her father's death, that brought her at forty to a conversion of seriousness, and then to the reform of her Order. At first she wanted just one reformed house where she could live as her inner life, which by this time was that of a mystic, dictated. Had she been a man, and elsewhere, one may speculate that she would have withdrawn into a hermitage. Her new house began with thirteen nuns, and in her remaining years she founded sixteen more. She was by no means unhumorous about her subjects. "I have always found that the best thing for broody nuns," she wrote, "is to make them dig." Her regime included a lot of manual work, for herself as well as the others, and it had the advantage of protecting the financial independence and therefore the poverty of her houses, though they did also accept alms. She required some intelligence and maturity from the nuns she admitted, and her common sense was robust. "God preserve me from stupid nuns!" She thought intelligent ones could better see and better amend their own faults of character. Her writings about prayer contain plenty of advice about the lower slopes, though she herself was undoubtedly a contemplative in the fullest sense. Her classic statement of the nature of contemplation is called *The Interior Castle*.

By contrast, it is instructive to remember Héloïse and Abelard. He had been the brightest scholar in Europe, in my view at least, and they were both by any standard brilliant. He was one of the finest Latin poets of the Middle Ages, to put it no higher, and a prose writer who can still hold one's attention. She was in many ways his equal, and they had been lovers. He was ruined, and they withdrew into monastic orders. The letters of Héloïse to Abelard were written when she was a famous abbess at a house called the Paraclete, which went on to become the core of a small new Order. Abelard was a rather unsuccessful abbot, poor fellow. She wrote to him that her love for him was as intense as ever, and she went over the whole relationship; the letters are very moving. She asked him to write a rule for her nuns, and to fill up the gaps in the Rule of Benedict by writing specially for women. She told him what subjects needed regulation. She wanted the freedom of a convent not visited by people of the world. She thought Benedict was silly to allow fish and not meat, since fish is more expensive and often more luxurious, and she thought wine ought to be forbidden, though women held their wine better than men did. Héloïse was not the only nun of her talent in the twelfth century; in Germany there were several. Abelard was unique, but he was not, alas, a canonizable saint. I do not expect he was a contemplative either, and nor was Héloïse. How would it have altered them, at that stage of their lives? Love at least is something they never lost.

Part 6

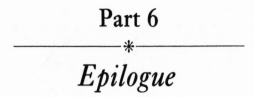

Epilogue

What Monks Symbolize

You can no more understand a medieval monastery by visiting a modern one than you can understand ancient architecture by wandering round Belgrave Square. The choice to be a monk today is far more gratuitous, far more against the grain of life, than it once was, and the revived monasteries of the British Isles are slightly coloured by the eccentricity of their nineteenth-century origins. Even in Continental Europe, where monastic tradition is more obviously continuous, there is something forlorn, something very slightly mad about monasteries. They are not central to our culture as they once were. When the Archbishop of Canterbury and the Dean invited the Ampleforth monks to sing the office in Westminster Abbey soon after the Archbishop's consecration, they were a surprising as well as a touching sight.

Yet whenever monasteries are stamped out, they seem to rise up again. This happens not only in Britain or Europe, and not only among Christians. When a Tang emperor confiscated the wealth and destroyed the institutions of Buddhist monks in China in 845, another emperor soon arose who refounded them. The religion of monks may have different origins and dogmas and expressions in different parts of the world, but one would suppose that Chinese and Indian and Tibetan and Christian monks must also have something in common. The bearded olive-farming monks of Athos differ from the original groups of Christian hermits in the Egyptian desert, and the abbot whom Tolstoy, who considered becoming a monk, consulted about his soul was unlike the great abbots of Tibet and Ladakh, whom he might have done better to consult; and yet a Tibetan lamaserai and a monastery on Athos have a similar look, and monks everywhere are accused of the same vices. Monasteries

dramatize the soul, at least for outsiders, and the ascent of the mind
to God. They seem to offer a mysterious union with God, a refreshment and peace of soul, and yet at the same time to withhold these
things from outsiders. Whether they exist for their own sake, for
the sake of the monks, or for the sake of what they mean to the rest
of us, is a question worth pursuing, and not so easily answered as it
seems. English monastic ruins are almost more impressive than a
living monastery; they are doubly dramatic. They pose formidable
questions about God and the soul, to which the light and shadows
of their ruined architecture offer the merest hints of answers. So
much blighted beauty is awe-inspiring. They are as unexplained
as Stonehenge, and the grass preaches as powerfully as the stones.
One wants to share in their massive darkness. When they were as
populous as ant-heaps and a central force in English economic life,
one might not have done so. The monastery is a refuge from the
world, a society of the good, and an assertion of the values of the
soul, but one might wish to take refuge even from a monastery, if
it were a successful institution.

What Survives

A few examples of most of the Western types of religious community
survive to this day. Apart from the continual movements of reform
and close discipline with written rules, the general tendency of the
later Middle Ages was towards good works and wandering monks
outside the cloister, and many religious orders that work in hospitals,
in cities, or for the poor, still exist, particularly for women. In third
world countries the missionary orders are still at work.

There are still a few hermits, though more in India than in
Europe. I do recollect a French hermit of Greek Orthodox faith in

a cave on the island of Patmos. His only books were Rimbaud and the Psalms. I had an English Dominican friend who lived a long time as a hermit in France; I had the impression that he was a mystic, and that his mystical calling drove him hard. I believe that the only purely contemplative Order today, existing for prayer and prayer alone, is a woman's order of perpetual adoration of the Blessed Sacrament, which they perform in shifts. They used to have a convent within sight of Marble Arch, which is the site of Tyburn, the place of execution of many Catholic saints.

The commonest Orders today are probably of missionaries, and of those who can flourish economically in the modern secular world. It is hard to believe that those country monasteries which make a living from the tourist trade, from coaches of visitors and awful little arts and crafts shops, can be very secure. But a school can make a living, and provide new recruits to the Order that runs it. Not that they all do so; I do not think many English boys ever joined the Irish brothers of the Christian Schools. The most successful recruiting grounds are the schools of those Orders not wholly committed to education, such as monastic and Jesuit schools, because they offer another dimension beyond the classroom. Women's Orders flourish at least equally with men's, and in much the same way, but for both men and women the increase in normal, secular education has brought a steep decrease in the number of religious recruits.

In the second half of this century the religious Orders all over Europe have lost much of whatever intellectual edge they had or seemed to have in the past. The approaches to mysticism are less innocent, and the subject matter of monastic and religious studies is paler-looking than it once was. Those who would once have gone to a religious Order now join some kind of peace corps or they join green earth groups, dabble in oriental religions or strange cults, or they become perpetual students or inward hermits. And yet monasteries do exist and quietly flourish, and the Rule of Benedict is still profoundly attractive to many. The nineteenth-century Trappist reform of the Cistercian Order is probably the austerest, because it combines life in close community with dead silence and constant penances. The Trappists have probably slowed down, but they have not yet run out of steam or relaxed their endeavours. It is rare to find durable recruits to the Carthusian Order, because of the peculiar combination of physical robustness and tolerance of solitude that the way of life demands, but recruits exist and probably always will. Of all the modern religious the Carthusians most uncompromisingly pursue a traditional life from the remote past. Their vocation, being mystical, is unaltered by historical change.

The Benedictines are much more recognizable as modern, both in the personal tone and quality of their vocations, and in their ease among outsiders. They still tend to inhabit large, unfunctional stone buildings like a cardboard mock-up of a late-medieval abbey. Indeed, wherever possible they like to take over medieval ruins and rebuild them. They take a pride in the "medieval" quality of their craftsmanship, and they tend towards stone-ground flour, pure farm food, and antiquarian peasant soup bowls. One expects to hear someone say "Pass the pipkin, brother". But their liturgy is solemn, faultless and profoundly peaceful. It is the centre of their lives and self-expression, and expresses the degree of their austerity. Once heard, it can never be forgotten. It is real, it is not play-acting.

A trickle of genuine vocations is still moving eastwards. I have an English friend whose cousin is the locally famous abbot of a non-Christian monastery in Pakistan. I think he was an Indian Army officer converted to Buddhism. The English monk Dom Bede Griffiths has been settled in saffron robes for many years, and has written much about Indian mysticism. He certainly has disciples. It is not just that the grass looks greener on the other side of the hedge. Monastic vocation is always to some degree a search for simplicity and pure origins, and in India those origins must surely seem closer than they do in most of modern Europe. The Himalayas are an inspiring sight. Andrew Harvey's book about Ladakh and its religious meaning for him (*Journey in Ladakh*, 1983) sets out the attraction graphically. One can feel it even in Kipling's *Kim*. The older Buddhist writings, for instance the ones in Edward

Conze's Penguin anthology (*Buddhist Scriptures*, 1959), are drenched in it.

And will you feel as a visitor today something of what was felt in the Middle Ages? Not unless you bring it with you. What you feel depends, of course, on what you are, and only if you could be as they were could you feel as they did. Today, if you shared the mind of the Middle Ages, that would be an elaborate and gratuitous choice; it would be a fantasy. As it is, the first and strongest sensation of a visitor is surprise. Then it is sensory deprivation: usually silence, no drink and no smoking. A new and strange daily rhythm asserts itself. One dreads the endless enchantment of church music, and the iron and apparently mindless repetition of the Scriptures. One is in the grip of slow rituals, and of emptiness. And in the end the life of the monastery enters into one's bones, after a week or two. If the visitor is a recruit the experience is different from all these. There will be a sense of opportunity, a certain excitement at having set out on a long journey, and at the same time a sense of coming home.

One of the greatest changes of the last forty years has been the introduction of English for the chanted office. Personally I find the new versions uncomforting, but I do not really think the monks and nuns mind very much what language they are talking. Those who underwent the change no doubt found for a time some new understanding, but by now the constant repetition of words will have given the sacred phrases a certain familiarity, a gloss or bloom. I have never in fact heard the whole office chanted in English by monks, but when I have heard any of it, the chant so dominated the language that I missed the Latin less than usual. The readings made more sense in English, though they were much less impressive than before. Or I was less impressionable.

Another recent change is that religious superiors have become since 1945 much more aware of psychology and psychiatry. The Pope had furious dealings some twenty years ago with a Benedictine house in Mexico that turned itself into a psychoanalytic centre on Freudian lines, with the abbot as head analyst. My own impression of theological training in the sixties was that the English Jesuit superiors would pack you off to a psychiatrist at the drop of a hat: a Catholic psychiatrist, of course. There are specialists and specialized clinics for the psychic troubles of religious. On the other hand there have always been wildly eccentric old and not so old men in religious houses, and that has not altered. They find a hole or a cranny from the world, they do some small job or other, and frequently give enormous pleasure to their brethren. The English Jesuits used to be proud of a particularly fine collection of extremely odd old men, and the longer established houses usually accumulated an underworld of crazy tramps and odd-looking labourers in addition. Everyone was very fond of them; one dreads the fate that awaits them in the cold hands of the modern world, now that such houses are rare. There must always have been people like that, dependent on monasteries, and the cultivation of mental health may be the mark of a harsher, less liberal attitude to them, whether they are clerical or lay.

The noviceship is a time when not so much the genuineness as the durability of a religious vocation is tested. A temporary enthusiasm can be genuine enough, but religious institutions insist on permanence and stability. One can see how this is in the interest of institutions, though its universal usefulness to individuals will to many appear more doubtful. It raises the most critical psychiatric question of all, whether the sense of religious vocation (which must include chastity) is not itself a psychic abnormality of clinical interest. One gets to know oneself very slowly in this world, and the ability to live one's life and to live with oneself cannot easily be predicted in advance. The number of vocations that a psychiatrist might have thought dangerous, but which in fact have turned out durable, flourishing, and creative of good, must be very great.

There do exist states of illusion or false vocation, though they can sometimes be diagnosed only in retrospect. One of the most frightening is the condition of some chaste young man who has an overwhelming experience of beauty and joy which he takes for the presence of God, though its real basis is simply the emergence of suppressed sexuality without an object. The psychic mechanism of artists is perhaps similar in origin, though that is much more bound up with techniques and technical achievement. The chaste young man's experience is almost ecstatic. His later experience when adolescence is over and he finds himself in his monastery will be a cumulative and bitter sense of loss, of the absence of the God of his youth. I have not invented this case; it was described at full clinical length in a journal, and I was given it to read by my novice master. It gave me such a fright that I have never forgotten it. The saddest cases are those like this one, that reveal themselves late in life, when it may be that life cannot cure them; neither the Order nor leaving the Order can cure them, and a psychiatrist must do his best.

Conclusion

In the study of monks and monasteries, no conclusion and many conclusions are possible. Readers must feel free to conclude as they wish. The subject extends so far in space, in different cultures and in historical time, that we must draw back from the trees in order to see the wood. It is generally true that monks are an elite, and that they can mostly read, they depend always on some kind of scriptures, which they can preserve and expound while the surrounding population is usually illiterate, or was so until recent times. It is also true that monks dramatize themselves and their vocation, communally or to one another, but also to the people around them. Their lives are ritualized. One of their most striking paradoxes among many is that monasteries are places of refuge, but monks are always in some way missionaries, and carry their scriptures with them to every new foundation.

Long ago it was an essential part of their calling to transmit and to produce written texts. In the West they had begun to lose this initiative by the thirteenth century, with the rise of reference books professionally produced, and the rise of universities. When printing was invented the younger Orders were swifter than the older ones to have presses of their own, and to put out new religious writings. From that time until the Benedictines of the late seventeenth century, monasteries made even fewer substantial contributions to learning than the Jesuits, who made few enough. The famous Armenian press at Venice was essentially an instrument of survival for a minority language among scattered communities; it expressed a sense of national identity in terms of religion and languages.

That language should be so very important in houses of silence is another paradox of monasteries. They are houses of the soul, and their deepest language comes from the depths of silence. But there are further paradoxes. By embracing a personal poverty which is close to being absolute the monk enters a world where he is richer than his cousins. By seeking peace and humility he enters an enclosed, protected place where his life is less troubled than other lives. By accepting his own death he may even contrive to live longer than the rest of his earthly family. By engaging himself in the discipline of obedience he frees himself from many worldly obligations and becomes almost invulnerable to earthly power. All this is as if monasteries were mankind's answer to the Beatitudes of Christ, a deliberate attempt to make them come true in an earthly way for monks and men. But of course the attempt is not a deliberate evasion, monasteries are not artificial paradises, and the demands of the Gospel are more searching and more intensely felt inside their walls than outside.

Some apprehended relation of time to eternity lies at the heart of their mystery. The Japanese priest Basho, speaking of his incessant pilgrimages, says that "As days and months are travellers through eternity, so I travel". Pilgrimage has been a more pronounced element in Buddhist monasticism than in the West, where Benedictine stability has prevailed, but some similar relation of time and eternity can be felt in all monastic cultures. A modern observer might imagine that eternity, an everlasting absolute moment as opposed to a triumphal procession of ages of ages, was a special illusion of monks, something they invented. As an idea it may well be a precondition of monasticism, but the monks did not invent it. The difference of pilgrimage and stability is much less important than this idea, and perhaps really arises from differences of climate.

Monasteries everywhere have a strong tendency to become lasting institutions, and to be built to last. This is not the same as being eternal, but it rests on a related idea of the permanence of books, permanent language, imperishable knowledge, and the permanence of divine worship by which the monastic community itself hopes for permanence. I take it that the palatial style of the older Oxford and Cambridge colleges, which were clearly built to last and often have a monastic appearance, derives from an overflow of the same view of things. But historical process and earthly activity do not stand still at the monastery gates. History has eroded the monasteries both from inside and from outside their walls, and it can never cease. Human societies alter in spite of themselves, just as individuals do. The clock never stops ticking, and the chimes of the monastery bells do no more than punctuate the ticking of the clock.

APPENDIX

Ruined Abbeys

That time of year thou may'st in me behold
When yellow leaves, or none, or few do hang
Upon those boughs that shake against the cold –
Bare ruin'd choirs where late the sweet birds sang.

Monastic limestone skeleton,
threadbare with simple love of life
speak out your dead language of stone,
the wind's hammer, the sun's knife,
the sweet apple of solitude;
there is a ninth beatitude:
a child in his simplicity
is more than a just man can be.
The idle ruins disregard
a chance human companion,
my words will make little mark on
limestone so jagged and so hard:
places essentially deserted
enchant only the single-hearted.
What are they, sprouting in the trees
dumb and so terrible to see?
What stony intellectual bees
could buzz among such fantasy?
And has my world travelled too far?
Watching all this in an armchair
consider what these ruins are,
desolate spirits in the air
singing in their stone languages
what religion is not and is,
not a museum but a stone
no man can understand alone:
what kind of spirit brought together
all these scattered arches and walls?

and what voice appeals and appalls,
weaving summer and winter weather
into the fabric of a vision,
a silent judge and no decision?

The face of all these stones is dead,
ruins petrify in the trees,
the tower glares like a bald head,
these dead abbeys are fantasies:
like terrible symbolic dreams
nourished on woods and stones and streams,
the dry voice of the river Styx.
Religion wears out its relics.
Their mouths are stone, their eyes are blind,
and who knows what they were saying?
Who can grasp this abandoned thing
pealing like thunder in my mind?
Sometimes I think it is a hymn
shouted by heavy seraphim.

And you might think walking in it
while the pillars move through your eyes
a life, a light seems to visit
a country where it calls and dies,
the truest silence is this noise,
how can that speak which has no voice?
Stone, wind and air without a sound
have risen speaking from the ground.
In the crude dark in the rank air
these clumsy harsh provincial stones
talk loud and clear as megaphones;
it is a virtue to despair
if human language is not this:
what heaven will be and earth is.

What is it in the eye and hand
that makes one thing out of another?
monasteries out of England,
a monk out of a human brother,
bread out of grain in the earth
or a young child out of a birth,
cloisters that could not last for long
from something resistant and strong.

Think what broods out in such a choice,
the ruin human minds intend,
what is this building in the end?
The stone's voice and the water's voice,
ragged walls in the tallest trees
predestined by my first wishes.

My work is like this after all,
to take new life out of a rhyme,
an hour of watch out of nightfall,
to make the day break from dead time,
so the sun's hand in the drowned grass
flashes a hundred panes of glass;
we rebuild night and thoughts of night
into a pyramid of light.
Absolute stillness occupies
the empty vaulted corridors,
the bare feet and the dusty floors
look like a criminal disguise
for secret thoughts and walking late
and that one thing I contemplate.

The pillars are rearing their weight,
the workmen's hands that lifted them
persist as force, to meditate
the discipline of the stone stem:
these stones were in their eyes and face,
their live bodies are this place:
honeycomb of shadows: a city
remote from terror and from pity;
look at the peaceful, soaring motion
like an unmotionable wave,
they never stir in their conclave,
they never speak in their devotion,
but the dead abbey still retains
the dead hand on the limestone reins.

Broken towers push their rough heads
where nothing can climb after them:
sheer arches rest on airy beds
the stone springs upward from the stem:
the eyesight of some holy man
is where this crumpled wall began,

vision and ruin seem the same:
ruin was his nature and name:
pillars like exploding rockets
that draped heaven or stained the moon,
the sting of dark, the swing of noon,
the sun itself and the planets
the empty heavens and the dove –
I understand nothing but love.

But who can understand heaven,
who understands peace of spirit?
What ignorant, what iron men
built this cold place so loving it?
The salmon leaping in his stream
can pull far stronger than a dream,
the black crow against the wind
can climb far higher than the mind.
Who is the man can set his face
to believe heaven will protect
a thing of his own intellect,
a thing of mass, shadow and space?
Confusions in the eye and heart
are where poems, not abbeys start.

The ruins wading through the grass
are like the ghost of Saint Bernard;
as if a thousand years must pass
and the stone face be deeper scarred
before it wakes like a wild creature
into the elements of nature,
might like a swan of heaven sing
its holy note only dying.

Think what brings an abbey to birth
from how deep in prehistory
it took the strong shape you can see,
it seems to have roots in the earth
leaves in the air: but the wind grieves,
it stands empty, there are no leaves.

Ruins are like a strong body
growing its strength in country air
then breeding age until you see

nettles are waving in its hair,
the ruined body keeps its shape
by the mechanics of landscape:
fox in the gorse, wind in the tree,
raincloud, fellside, mystery:
what was born wild is never tame:
ten numbers never written down
can make a spade a wall and a town,
fellsides and abbeys are the same:
until time draws like a deduction
true proportions for their destruction.

Water and stone, bracken and wood,
clouds in the sky, sheep on the fell
have transmuted the true and good:
look close at them and you can tell
the architecture that they like,
think how the sun and wind will strike
at truth and goodness in this shape,
hammering walls too tough to rape.
This world is like a window-pane,
age within age goes its own way:
fields of barley denser than hay
sweep up into long heads of grain
transmuted by his hands who said
the grain will die, my words are bread.

Unquarried rock carries the print
of prehistoric origins,
the burnt forest sleeps in the flint
and the worked stone builds the ruins;
what ice, what mountain weight of ice
compounded rock in this crevice?
What glacier groaned in the lock
to lock this strength into this rock?
Streaming with water, secretly
breathing the cold eating the sun
until its prison was undone
by Christ in the twelfth century,
this rock endured, and you can trace
the hurt hands in the quarried face.

Bones are a limestone but it bleeds,
a man is an imperfect stone,
what the unquarried limestone needs
is intellectual alone.
It can sing louder than a thrush
on the fellside in the rose-bush,
without a clapper like a bell,
as clear as Christ in the gospel:
all creatures breed with their own kinds,
and when this rock was remarried
Christ and the gospel blessed its seed
with *amor vincit*, love binds.
What is it in the marks you see
so moves you to morality?

Think how high a pillar can stand,
primitive art, a kind of zero,
still the work of somebody's hand:
a self-portrait, a limestone hero,
a fantasy drawn in the light,
expressing self-knowledge as height:
and stone on stone: – this discipline
has a deep limestone origin.

Only the virgin stone knows why
the arches swing against the sky.
We use ruins for idle time
to take a bath in the sublime.

This abbey was what the tree is
and the column is natural,
now its branches are silences:
e'en let it stand till it down fall.
Angels like birds caught in mid-flight
were incoherent at twilight;
birds are dead meteors, this age
puts out no stony foliage,
but my face is a figurehead
split by the weather in the south,
the stone ivy twines in my mouth,
angels are finished, birds are dead:
and yet the ivy on the tree
is my life, is what I shall be.

Deep in the woods masses of leaves
live as no abbey is alive,
the unprinted sunrise receives
its praise only from crops that thrive.
Monasteries in their November
can only mumble and remember
this sharpness in the life and sense:
life is some kind of innocence.
Natural uses and abuses
eat down the forest in the end,
and only stone is the stone's friend,
distilling solitary juices:
heaven revives and lives forever,
the end of religion is never.

Night stalks through the ruins.
Moonlight and dusk handle relics.
The river remembers its sins.
Things interpenetrate and mix.

The old sunk ship rises up high
disturbing birds in the black sky.
You are yourself at night, prophetic
in your nature, and sympathetic
to forgotten laws of childhood,
night is your natural limit,
this body of darkness in it
is your extreme of solitude.
The abbey at night is a king,
an unexampled, solemn thing.

And this darkness never deludes.
It is original justice,
the Buddha of these solitudes;
riches too cold for avarice.
This is the original mark.
Monks like bees buzzed in the dark,
they were moths in a black forest
where the tree-sugar ran truest.
This is intellectual light:
day-working and night-waking,
the psalms sung with their eyes aching

the human darkness and midnight:
the bees of darkness in the hive
of light when the light was alive.

An absence and a poverty:
a certain simple understanding
of what a man is or will be,
ears and eyes for the one commanding
face with the gaze of fire that looks
out from the first Christian books.
Something human opens at night
and grows slowly towards the light.
It dawns. Birds call for daybreak,
stop singing, and the world's awake.

Bread of heaven, heavenly light
shake away sleep from my eyes,
make the sun flame, the day be bright,
O light, O darkness of the wise.
This abbey is stones and ashes;
I no longer know what it is.
Dead monuments. An extinct fire.
It has neither voice nor desire.
Say at one particular moment
which old history had prepared
and many generations shared
this abbey element by element
was desecrated beyond all mention
and the fire smothered and the hearth pissed on.

Try; break the walls up in your head,
let cattle-urine splash the chrism,
see the place well desecrated,
safe for art history and capitalism;
and then remember in the end
that all of this really happened.
But that the intonation of the wind
is savage, and it is not in the mind.
We live at the whole world's expense,
we live in debt, what was rejected
can not ever be resurrected.
Never. There is no innocence.
In this generations will share:
a dead abbey is a nightmare.

Look at this and be terrified,
it was not the judgement of God,
it was not sloth, or wealth, or pride,
but a choice taken and followed.

Peace is a bird in mid-heaven
that can be known by lonely men.
This lonely and abandoned house
whose voices no voice can arouse
visited for an hour or two
will say in Latin *meditate*,
and recites phrases like *too late*
to those who know what they should do.
Well, forget the abandoned crime:
live better in the present time.

What is it then, a human
life, human society?
The Bible says four streams ran
from paradise; where are we?
Body, spirit, Holy Ghost,
the language is dumb almost.
Who really knows his origin
or whose image we are made in?
Adam was sweating and digging
three centuries in paradise;
I sweat and dig for the same price,
and sing as loud as the birds sing;
but this is not the first garden;
monastic heaven is broken.

When Adam worked in the sun
his tree was lost, he hated light,
he loved shade, so he grew one
like a fresh garden of delight:
Adam was nine hundred and blind
when this great tree grew in his mind.
All those paradises are over.
Work goes on. There is no cover.
I have this simple attitude:
God gives the tree, waters the root,
God gives the tree and the fruit,

the fresh apple of solitude.
Say what is a human spirit?
God gives the bread that feeds it.

Spirit in heaven, white dove
inspire what God has created,
with water-springs of heaven's love
till soberly intoxicated
I can see my own origin,
the unknown image I am in.
The dove of heaven is alone,
his breasts are water his voice stone,
once in history he defied
nature and man for a virgin
building his streams for ever in
the snowy heaven of her side;
every monk and abbey is
a kind of monument of this.

It ends in death, the old land.
Darkness climbs into the sky.
There is nothing left in your hand.
It gives you no guide to go by.
Or nothing that a stinging-nettle
on a bleak stone will not unsettle.
You who believe my true story
are not protected from history.
What can I say about death;
their death is hidden from my eyes:
but I believe that the dead rise,
having been roused by the strong breath
of my God who is in heaven,
when the trumpet tears earth open.

Before they died death was present,
in such a death all life survives,
this is to die human and content,
at peace and delightful in their lives:
and there was nothing lamentable,
even death can be serviceable.
Under the earthly limestone crown
in grave after grave they lay down.

APPENDIX

Here death was never quite at home,
in fields not chosen for dying
they simply slept and lie sleeping
and shall lie till the crack of doom.
And I hope to be one who dies
with simple ruins in his eyes.

Water is running in my head
cold as the water from Christ's side,
cold as the voices of the dead
and of those who have never died,
they live in words, they are still speaking,
they have found what I have been seeking.
Ailred of Rievaulx and Bernard,
was it only on wood so hard
your ripe, sound apples could grow?
Under the coarseness of time
under lichen, rain, grime,
ruins are all that I know:
and your words speaking from the page;
the Word is in words, age after age.

The rain has blotted out the stone.
Try to understand its message.
I take the stone's life for my own
these ruins for a hermitage:
here I shall contemplate that truth
which must consume my age and youth,
and put words to that only good
that chimes so well with solitude.
The foolish letters of poor names
are written on this holy stone,
but reading them I am at one
with the Arabian bird in flames:
death in the amber-weeping tree
whose life is what my life shall be.

(for a BBC film of Cistercian ruins in Yorkshire, 1966)

SUGGESTED READING

Alexander, M., *Old English Literature* (Macmillan, 1983)

Basho, M., *The Narrow Road to the Deep North and other Travel Sketches* (Penguin Books, 1970)

Birch, C. (ed.), *Penguin Anthology of Chinese Literature* (Penguin Books, 1965)

Brenan, G., *St John of the Cross: His Life and Poetry* (Cambridge University Press, 1973)

Brooke, C., *Monasteries of the World* (Omega, 1982)

Conze, E. (ed.), *Buddhist Scriptures* (Penguin Books, 1959)

Farmer, H. (ed.), *The Oxford Dictionary of Saints* (Oxford University Press, 1978)

Fermor, P. L., *A Time to Keep Silence* (John Murray, 1982)

Godman, P., *Poetry of the Carolingian Renaissance* (Duckworth, 1982)

Hobson, A., *Great Libraries* (Weidenfeld & Nicolson, 1970)

Knowles, D., *Bare Ruined Choirs: the Dissolution of the English Monasteries* (Cambridge University Press, 1976)

— *Monastic Britain* (map, Ordnance Survey, n.d.)

— *Religious Orders in England* (3 vols., Cambridge University Press, 1979)

Knowles, D. and Hadcock, R., *Medieval Religious Houses in England and Wales* (Longman, 1971)

Lawrence, C. H., *Medieval Monasticism: Forms of Religious Life in Western Europe in the Middle Ages* (Longman, 1984)

Mathew, G., *Byzantine Aesthetics* (John Murray, 1963)

Matthiessen, P., *Nine-Headed Dragon River: Zen Journals 1969–1982* (Collins Harvill, 1986)

Nicol, D. M., *Meteora: Rock Monasteries in Thessaly* (Variorum, 1975)

Spelman, Sir Henry, *The History and Fate of Sacrilege, with an Introductory Essay by Two Priests of the Church of England* (2nd edn., 1853)

Sullivan, M., *The Cave Temples of Maichishan* (Faber & Faber, 1969)

Thomas, C., *Early Christian Archaeology of Northern Britain* (Oxford University Press, 1971)

Walters, C. C., *Monastic Archaeology in Egypt* (Aris and Phillips, 1974)

The following books appeared too late for me to consult them:

Rodley, L., *Cave Monasteries of Byzantine Cappadocia* (Cambridge University Press, 1986)

Rousseau, P., *Pachomius* (University of California Press, 1986)

INDEX